The miracles of Jesus were the ordinary works of His Father, wrought small and swift that we might take them in.

GEORGE MACDONALD

Nature and Altering It

Allen Verhey

William B. Eerdmans Publishing Company

Grand Rapids, Michigan / Cambridge, U.K.

Published 2010 by

Wm. B. Eerdmans Publishing Co.

2140 Oak Industrial Drive N.E., Grand Rapids, Michigan 49505 /

P.O. Box 163, Cambridge CB3 9PU U.K.

Printed in the United States of America

16 15 14 13 12 11 10   7 6 5 4 3 2 1

Library of Congress Cataloging-in-Publication Data

Verhey, Allen.

Nature and altering it / Allen Verhey.

p.   cm.

ISBN 978-0-8028-6548-9 (pbk.: alk. paper)

1. Nature — Religious aspects — Christianity.

2. Human ecology — Religious aspects — Christianity.   I. Title.

BT695.5.V45   2010

261.8′8 — dc22

2010015111

www.eerdmans.com

Contents

Contents

Preface

It was a great honor to give the 2008 Jellema Lectures at Calvin College. It was a great honor because I am an alumnus of Calvin College and Seminary — but not just because of that. It was a great honor because William Harry Jellema was the beloved colleague of my own beloved teacher and mentor at Calvin College and Seminary, Henry Stob — but not just because of that. It was a great honor because Professor Jellema taught and mentored a series of Calvin students who went on to make outstanding contributions as Christian philosophers, including Alvin Plantinga and Nicholas Wolterstorff — but not just because of that. It was a great honor because, although I never had a class with Professor Jellema, I count him among my teachers at Calvin College. He was a mentor I never met.

In the little book that shaped the vision of Calvin College, *The Curriculum in a Liberal Arts College,* Professor Jellema complained about an education that had as its objective "the [student's] ability so to use nature as to achieve position in a society devoted to mastery over nature."[1] He urged instead an education that had as its objective the formation of a Christian "Mind," a mind deeply formed and informed by the Christian tradition and ready to meet and to challenge the other "Minds" at work in culture.

I wanted the lectures to honor W. Harry Jellema by honoring that agenda. The topic for the lectures was that "mastery over nature" to which this society is still devoted, and my hope was that they might help to form a Christian "Mind" on "nature and altering it." This little book is a revision and expansion of those lectures. It focuses on "nature" and our ecological responsibilities. But because it wants to avoid romantic accounts of nature, it also attends to some other responsibilities and to some warrants for "altering nature."

The book begins by acknowledging that "nature" is a slippery word. Because it means quite different things to different people, the first chapter attempts to sort out some of the different meanings of "nature." The chapter ends, however, by acknowledging that such a philological exercise does not get us very far. It gets us only this far: to the recognition that the meaning of "nature" depends on the context provided by a narrative, by a "myth." So the second chapter turns to an effort to identify and to question some of the myths at work in our culture, myths that have formed the "Mind" of modernity and its fundamental perspectives on nature and altering it. Because those myths are ripe for doubt, the book will turn to Christian Scripture for an alternative story, a story capable of challenging the dominant myths and capable of forming a different ethos concerning nature and altering it. But be-

1. William Harry Jellema, *The Curriculum in a Liberal Arts College* (Grand Rapids: Calvin College, 1958).

cause it is precisely the Christian story that has sometimes been accused of nurturing arrogance concerning nature, it will be necessary in the third chapter first to respond to that accusation and to clear the way for a fresh look at the biblical narrative. The fourth chapter attempts to provide that fresh reading of the biblical story and to attend to the ways in which that story locates us and orients us within the creation. If it is successful, it will allow Scripture to re-form our perspective on nature and on altering it. But because narrative is not sufficient, it will be necessary in a concluding chapter to suggest some of the ways in which the biblical story can fund other forms of moral discourse. That last chapter will necessarily be suggestive rather than exhaustive, but I hope to display something of the relevance of the biblical narrative to these other important forms of moral discourse. The narrative can fund a contemporary prophetic voice. It can echo in the voice of the contemporary ecological sage. It can be instructive for the analytical discourse that nurtures moral clarity. And it is relevant to the political discourse of policy makers, even if it cannot be directly translated into policy. A community of moral discourse and deliberation and discernment still requires all of those voices speaking to each other and listening to each other. And Christian discernment still requires that we test the reasons given and heard by the story Christians still delight to tell and still struggle to perform. Both Christian churches and Christian colleges are called to be such communities of discourse. This little book is not intended to be a substitute for that communal discourse and discernment, but it does hope to make a small contribution to it.

It hopes to make that contribution by nurturing a "Mind" formed and informed by the Christian story and capable of meeting and challenging the "Minds" that shape our culture's attitudes to nature and altering it.

I thank the Philosophy Department of Calvin College and especially Lee Hardy for the invitation to give the Jellema Lectures and for warm hospitality and good conversation. The Jellema Lectures themselves represented a reworking of material I had prepared for an interdisciplinary dialogue sponsored by the Ford Foundation and led by Baruch Brody, B. Andrew Lustig, and Gerald McKenny. I had the benefit in that context of dialogue with a distinguished group of interdisciplinary scholars interested in both ecology and in genetics, assisted reproductive technologies, and other ways of "altering nature." My thanks to the Ford Foundation and to my colleagues in that conversation. I want also to thank Stephen R. Graham, then Dean of Faculty and Academic Life at North Park College, for the invitation to give the Lund Lectures there. One of those lectures was an early draft of what became the Jellema Lectures and this little book.

Finally, I want to thank Ellen Davis for reading an earlier draft of this material and Andy Lustig and Elizabeth Sudduth for their comments on the penultimate draft of this book.

I

"Nature": What Is It?
Sixteen Senses and Still Counting

I f we are to think about "nature" and about "altering it," it would be good to know what we are thinking about, what "nature" is. But "nature" turns out to mean many different things. Following C. S. Lewis's wonderful philological exercise in *Studies in Words*,[1] I undertook the task of listing some

1. C. S. Lewis, *Studies in Words,* 2nd ed. (Cambridge: Cambridge University Press, 1967). The pages in parentheses are references to this work. Many others, of course, have observed the different ways in which "nature" is understood and used. Paulos Gregorios, *The Human Presence: An Orthodox View of Nature* (Geneva: World Council of Churches, 1978), for example, identifies five different concepts of nature: 1) what happens without human interference, 2) the non-human part of the creation, 3) what is beyond the reach of human agency (that is, nature in contrast to history and culture), 4) what is not beyond the reach of ordinary human powers (that is, nature in contrast to the supernatural or to grace), and 5) the character or structure of a thing, the kind of thing a thing is. "[I]t is," he says, "the very concept of nature itself that is problematic" (p. 17). See also Gordon Kaufmann, "A Problem for Theology: The Concept of Nature," *Harvard Theological Review* 65 (1972): 337-66, where three basic concepts are identi-

of the different senses of "nature." The list quickly grew to sixteen. The task grew tiresome as the senses multiplied, and I left the task unfinished, still counting. Even so, the list provides a convenient place to begin and may provide some clarity along the way.

"Nature" #1: Like us, the Greeks used "nature" *(phusis)* quite often and quite unselfconsciously to mean *the kind of thing a thing is.* In one of his famous definitions, Aristotle says, "whatever each thing is like when its process of coming-to-be is complete, that we call the nature [the *phusis*] of each thing" *(Politics* 1252b, cited in Lewis, p. 34). That's the sort of thing anything is, Aristotle thought, the kind of thing it grows into. The Latin *natura* and the English "nature," like the Greek *phusis,* frequently have this meaning: the sort or kind of thing a thing is, the character of a thing.

"Nature" #2: Even before Aristotle, however, *phusis* had come to mean something else, something more. It came to mean *"everything."* The pre-Socratics thought it would be useful to capture all the things they knew — minerals, plants, animals, human beings, gods — under a single name, and for some reason the name they gave to this heterogeneous collection of things into a single object of study was *phusis,* or "nature" (Lewis, p. 35). Parmenides' work, "On Nature" *(Peri Phusis),* for example, was a work about "everything," and may well mark the linguistic invention of this sense of "nature." This sense of "nature," however, could not accomplish much. Strictly speaking, "nature" in this sense has no opposite. Moreover, not much can be finally

---

fied: "the essential qualities or properties" of a thing, "the totality of powers and processes that make up the universe," and "that which exists independently of all human artifice."

said about "everything." And to be told that something is a part of "nature" in this sense is not to learn anything more about it.

"Nature" #3, #4, #5, and #6: This invention of a new sense of "nature" did produce important reactions — and additional senses of "nature." Some said that these older thinkers had not given an account of everything, after all. There was something more. They might have said, I suppose, that *phusis* contains more than the older thinkers thought, but instead they said that there was something more than *phusis* (Lewis, p. 37). "Nature" was in a sense demoted, at least restricted. "Nature" was not "everything" but *"everything but. . . ."* Plato, for example, who thought everything in the perceptible universe to be only an imitation and a product of the imperceptible and timeless "forms," used "nature" (nature #3) quite naturally for the whole perceptible universe, for "everything but . . ." the forms (which were, in his view, more real and more valuable than everything else). For his part, Aristotle demoted or restricted "nature" to that which is subject to change (nature #4), and he studied those things in what he called "natural philosophy." But there is more — and more to study. There are those things that are unchangeable but cannot exist "on their own." These things were studied in mathematics. And there is one thing that is unchangeable but can exist "on its own," namely God, the unmoved mover. Christianity and Judaism and Islam, of course, also insisted that there was something more than *phusis*. There is God. Moreover, this God is related to "everything" as creator. "Nature" is the work of God, God's creation, "everything but . . ." God (nature #5). Eventually "nature" was demoted or restricted even more, to refer to something less than the whole created world, to everything "under the moon" but not to the sky (nature #6).[2]

"Nature" #7: Besides these restrictions and demotions, however, there was also *an apotheosis* of "nature" (Lewis, p. 40). This was hardly possible before "nature" had been named. But once named, "nature" could be personified and was. "Nature" was raised to divinity, to the sense of Great Mother Nature. To be sure, it is difficult sometimes to decide whether the personified "nature" names a deity or is understood as a rhetorical figure. At any rate, "nature" does come to have this sense sometimes, not just "everything" but a divine force or mind taken to be immanent in everything. When Stoics like Marcus Aurelius called *Phusis* "the eldest of deities" (*Meditations* IX, I), it sounds like religion. And this sense of Great Mother Nature has resisted dismissal. We still talk of "she" who "abhors a vacuum," is "red in tooth and claw," eliminates the unfit, moves toward higher forms of life, warns, comforts, teaches, and so on.

Meanwhile, we also go on using "nature" in other ways — to identify the kind of thing a thing is, or in one of the restricted senses we have observed, or in some other sense still. The list of the meanings of "nature" grows if we consider the implied opposites of "natural."

"Nature" #8: The "natural" can be contrasted, of course, with the "unnatural." This sense may be dependent upon nature #1, the sort of thing a thing is, the "unnatural" marking a departure from the sort of thing a thing is but also — and curiously — marking it as bad. "Natural" then comes to mean not

2. Aristotle, *Metaphysics* 1072b, says that upon God "the sky and all *phusis* depend," words echoed by Dante in *Paradiso* XXVIII, 41, and registered in Chaucer's phrase "under the moon" in "The Physician's Tale" (Lewis, pp. 39, 40).

only fitting to the sort of thing that a thing is but also *"good"* (nature #8). But as C. S. Lewis observed, "when the timid man forces himself to be brave, . . . he is not called *unnatural"* (p. 43).

"Nature" #9: The "natural" can otherwise be contrasted with "the interfered with." It is a commonplace sense, invoked usually by the adverb "naturally," that is to say, "if *not interfered with,*" "if left alone" (p. 44). The sense of "nature" here is *"the given,"* or "the unaltered" (nature #9). It is easy enough to identify this sense, but not so easy to explain how we got to it. Perhaps we got to it because we assumed that the sort of thing a thing is (nature #1) will eventually emerge if the thing is not interfered with. But one might as easily observe that the nature of nature is constant and reciprocal interference. That is to say, the sort of thing (nature #1) "everything" is — whether in a restricted sense or not (whether nature #2, #3, #4, #5, or #6) — is that things are constantly interfered with by other things.

Nature #9 can easily accommodate the personification of a force immanent in everything (nature #7), as when we say, "It's not nice to fool with Mother Nature," but it does not seem to require it. It does, however, seem to require a contrast between humanity and nature that we have not yet encountered in this philological exercise — and, indeed, a contrast that would be denied by nature #1, #2, #3, #4, #5, and #6. The interference being thought about, after all, is usually interference by human beings. To beavers, one might suppose, the dam in the stream would be an interference, "unnatural," and the paved road by the side of the stream, what is given, or "nature." But to human beings the beavers' dam seems to be nature (nature #9), and the paved road, an intervention into what is given. Perhaps we could say that it is the nature (nature #1) of human beings to interfere with what is given (nature #9), but it is the nature of almost everything to interfere with what is given.

"Nature" #10: As we have just observed, nature #9 seemed to require a contrast between humanity and nature that we had not previously noted. We must pause to note, therefore, this still more restricted use of "nature," "nature" demoted to *"everything but . . . humanity"* (nature #10). It can be found in this sense in Wordsworth and in most "nature poets" (Lewis, p. 73).

"Nature" #11: Sometimes, however, the line is drawn not between nature and humanity but between features or elements of our humanity. Sometimes, as in the phrase "nature calls," nature includes part of our humanity, the animal part. Some other part, the rational part or the spiritual part or the soul, for example, is marked off from nature. Nature, then, is *"everything but . . . some part of a human being"* (nature #11). Then the nature of the human being, the sort of thing a human being is (nature #1), would be part nature (nature #11) and part not. Moreover, it might then be regarded as part of the nature of the human being (nature #1) to alter nature, to interfere with "the given" (nature #9), at least by restraining the animal or the "natural" part of a human being (nature #11). Such interference, furthermore, might be approved or deplored. If the interference is deplored, then "nature" or "the natural" would be presumed "good" (nature #8). If it is approved, then "nature" or "the natural" would be presumed to be the raw or the savage or the "beast" in us. Confusing enough, I suppose, but we are not quite done with the list.

"Nature" #12: The "natural" may also be contrasted with the civil. Consider Aristotle's claim that some are "natural slaves."³ Presumably he meant that it was the nature (nature #1) of some to be slaves, that that was the sort of thing some people simply were. Now one should object, of course, that it is not the nature (nature #1) of any human being to be a slave. But leaving that aside, one might also object that a particular slave was not a slave by "nature" but by law or convention. The Greek and Macedonian slave trade was not very good, I suspect, at ensuring that only natural slaves would be enslaved. But if Aristotle's society was to lay claim to being just, it would have to distinguish the one who was a slave by nature from the one who was a slave simply by law or convention, and it would have to free the latter. The contrast, of course, concerns not just slaves, but the legislation and administration of the society more generally. The contrast is between the law and what is "really right" (Lewis, p. 59). What is "really right" may be regarded, of course, as "the laws of the gods, unwritten and unvarying,"⁴ but it can also be regarded as the "law of nature" (Lewis, p. 60). "Nature" in such contexts and in such contrasts means the *"really right"* (nature #12), independent of civil law, indeed, the final test for civil legislation and administration. Ancient, medieval, and early modern thinkers invoked "nature" in moral and political philosophy — but the ambiguities of "nature" permitted quite different uses of "nature" in political philosophies.

"Nature" #13 and #14: For the Stoics, for example, the laws of nature were the laws of Mother Nature (nature #7). For Christians, God had inscribed God's laws on human hearts, on human nature (nature #1), and on the whole creation (nature #5). There surely may be a place reserved for personified

---

3. See the discussion of slavery in Aristotle, *Politics,* Book I, iv-vi.
4. Sophocles, *Antigone,* 453, cited by Lewis, p. 59.

Nature in God's heavenly court, but she is there under the authority of God, and she learns her laws from God. For both Stoics and Christians, however, the laws of nature are "really right." For Hobbes, on the other hand, the laws of nature were simply the way human beings (and all other living beings) "naturally" behaved if there were no interference (nature #9), and in Hobbes's vision and philosophy "the law of nature" was simply to act in self-preservation and self-interest. It is not what is "really right" (nature #12); it is "the given" (nature #9).

For both Hobbes and the Stoics the contrast between the laws of nature and civil laws remains, but the contrast is assessed quite differently. In Hobbes, of course, in the "state of nature" human life was "solitary, poor, nasty, brutish, and short."[5] The "given," the "natural," is violence, a state of savagery that civil law enables us to escape but to which we are always at risk of descending again. On the other hand, among Stoics and Christians the "state of nature" was frequently regarded as a state of "peaceable difference," as a time of innocence, from which humanity has somehow fallen. Consider Seneca's claim that "the first of mortals and their children followed nature, uncorrupted, and enjoyed the nature of things [nature #2] in common."[6] Or Pope's couplet, "Nor think in Nature's state they blindly trod, / The state of Nature was the reign of God."[7] The Stoics and Hobbes have obviously quite different accounts of the "state of nature," quite different (and contradictory) senses of "nature" itself. For Hobbes, nature is *the arena of violence* (nature #13), and

---

5. Thomas Hobbes, *Leviathan,* ed. J. C. A. Gaskin (Oxford: Oxford University Press, 1996), 13.9.

6. *Epistle* XC, 4, 18, cited by Lewis, p. 62.

7. *Essay on Man* III, 147, cited by Lewis, p. 63.

for the Stoics, nature is *the arena of peaceable difference* (nature #14).[8]

Nature #15: The task grows tiresome; the senses multiply. But we should note also the contrast of the "natural" and the "supernatural." "Supernatural," of course, may be applied to a wide variety of phenomena, to ghosts as well as gods, to miracles as well as almost anything mysterious. What binds these phenomena together as "supernatural" seems to be their power to evoke some sense of awe. But what sort of contrast is this? Isn't the "natural" itself, the starry heavens, for example, capable of evoking some sense of awe? Does that make the "natural" itself "supernatural"? In Christian theology it makes good sense, of course, to speak of the "supernatural." The power of God sometimes lifts a human being (or some other being) to do that which is above or beyond its own powers, given the sort of thing it is (nature #1). We name such times miraculous or "supernatural." But, again, what sort of contrast is this? In Christian theology it is the power of God that also gives a human being (and all other things) the power to do what is within its own powers, given the sort of thing it is. The birth of a child is still miraculous. We are on a dangerous path if we allow this contrast of the "natural" and the "supernatural" to empty the world of wonder, if we use it to define a miracle simply as a contradiction of nature, or if we understand "nature" itself as *without God* and the power of God (nature #15). Science may indeed say many true and im-

8. It could be noted that this contrast between natural and civil, or between natural law and civil law, or between the state of nature and civil government, can be transposed — and frequently has been — to a contrast between natural and civilized. But such a contrast closely resembles the contrast between nature #9, the given, and the interference wrought by the practical arts exercised by humanity.

portant things about nature without using God as a hypothesis, but all that it says should nurture a sense of awe, not just a hope for mastery.

Nature #16: Christian theology has complicated things still more, distinguishing human "nature" as created from our human "nature" as fallen and by insisting that we can hardly make sense of human nature, of the sort of creature human beings are (nature #1) without attending both to God's creation and to human sin. Both "natures" in our nature may have their laws, but these laws are at war with one another (Rom. 7:23). And to complicate matters still more in Christian theology, "nature," whether created or fallen, may be contrasted with "grace." But again, we may ask what sort of contrast this is, a question that has prompted no shortage of theological reflection. Does grace contradict nature? Or fulfill it? Is it added to nature? Or is it the foundation of nature? It makes a difference, of course, if we are considering our nature as created or as fallen, but every concrete human being is both created and fallen. It is grace that made us, grace that sustains us in spite of our sin, and grace that makes things, all things, new. We are on another dangerous path if we allow this contrast of the "nature" and "grace" to empty "nature" of grace, as if "nature" could be understood, even if we have not forgotten the power of God, as *without the grace of God* (nature #16).

The reader is surely as tired of this list-making as I am. We leave it aside, still counting. Three conclusions from this list, however, are surely warranted. First, although the context usually clarifies the particular sense of "nature" being used, there are possibilities of confusion here. "Nature" is a slippery word. It is possible, for example, to confuse "the given" (nature #9) and the "really right" (nature #12). The risks of confusion exist both in discourse among people and in one's own deliberation. If there is a remedy for confusion, it will be some greater clarity and consistency about the sense of "nature" that is invoked.

Second, there are choices to be made — and somehow defended. Should we regard nature as "everything" or as somehow restricted and demoted? If we should regard it as somehow restricted, what is left out of its borders? Does nature include humanity or not? And if it does, what is the place of humanity within it? What is the appropriate human attitude toward nature? And what is the appropriate human vocation with respect to it? Should nature be personified and apotheosized or disenchanted? Should it be regarded as raw and savage, as dangerous and oppressive, or as innocent and peaceable?

The third conclusion, however, and perhaps the most important, is that none of these questions can be answered by the sort of philological archaeology that we have so far engaged in. This little philological exercise has only displayed that answers to such questions are required and that the answers will always be embedded in larger visions, in "metaphysics,"[9] if you like, or in myth.

To think about nature and altering it, to deliberate about human responsibility *for* nature (or, perhaps, about human responsibility *to* Mother Nature) will demand that we attend to myth or to something akin to myth. The very concept of

9. I mean a modest "metaphysics," the sort captured by Aristotle's order if not by his practice. His works were usually arranged in this order: the *Organon* (or tool, works on logic), the *Phusika* (scientific works on nature), *ta meta ta phusika* ("the things after the *phusika*," the metaphysics; works on God, unity, being, cause, potentiality), and finally works on human practices *(Ethics, Politics, Rhetoric, Poetics).*

"nature" is itself almost always embedded in a larger vision that will require the scrutiny of Christians. Indeed, insofar as the concept of "nature" is sometimes taken to imply something autonomous and independent of God, some Christian theologians have rejected the concept of "nature" in favor of the concept of "creation." Joseph Sittler has made this point.[10] He continues to use the word "nature," of course, but he construes it as "creation." And so shall we.

For the sake of some initial clarity, then, let me stipulate that I am using "nature" in the fifth sense, as the creation, as everything but . . . God, the creator. And let me also identify the myth, or the thing akin to myth, that should form a Christian "Mind" about these matters: the story given in Christian Scripture. Before I turn to the Christian story, however, permit me to call attention in the next chapter, both to the importance of myth and to some of the myths that have shaped our minds and our relationship to nature but that are ripe for doubt.

10. Joseph Sittler, *Essays on Nature and Grace* (Philadelphia: Fortress, 1972), p. 99. See also Robert Quam, "Creation or Nature? A Manner of Speaking," *Word and World* 11 (Spring 1991): 147-55. I am indebted for these citations — and for much more — to my colleague Steven Bouma-Prediger. See his work *The Greening of Theology* (Atlanta: Scholars Press, 1995), pp. 274-303. Gordon Kaufmann has also argued that "nature" frequently has an "implicit metaphysic" and that "the concept will have to be subjected to careful scrutiny" because "the metaphysical tendencies implicit in it are not obviously congruent with those of the Christian faith." Kaufmann, pp. 347-48. See also Paulos Gregorios, *The Human Presence,* pp. 21-23.

II

"Every Ethos *Implies a* Mythos*"*

I t was Aristotle's claim that character development (or *ethos*) requires a plot (or *mythos*).[1] It is not just a point in literary theory. I take it also to be true of moral development and of moral discernment. Discernment of our human responsibilities requires a myth.

It is important, of course, to explain the term *myth*. It is another slippery word. It is used popularly and pejoratively to refer to a story that is not true, a story that can be refuted by science. I use it quite differently here. To quote the Catholic scholar, H. Fries, myth may better be regarded as

> characterized by the fact that it sees the empirical world and its happenings, and above all, man and his action, in the light of the reality that constitutes them, and makes them a unity, and at the same time transcends them. . . . It is mostly in narrative form, a story which is "sacred word" . . . a word about true being and the all-

---

1. *Poetics* 1450a.15-1450b.4.

[13]

sustaining event, not merely in the causal sense, but in the sense that it gave meaning and purpose to all actual being and happenings.[2]

Myths help us to map our world and our place in it. They serve to orient us, to locate us; they enable us to interpret and to see the significance of the things and events around us. Without some such map we are lost. Without some such story or drama that gives meaning and purpose, we do not know what role we are to play or what character we need for it. "Every *ethos* requires a *mythos.*"

Myth is inescapable, even for those who would debunk myths. Jacques Monod is a case in point. In *Chance and Necessity* he wants to convince his readers that nature is "objective," by which he means that it has no values or purposes. Everything in it, he says, is "contingent," by which he means that all the items in it are unconnected except by "chance." Leave aside for a moment that this way of picturing the universe relies on the (once popular) myth of separate and impenetrable atoms. Leave aside the fact that relations are much more interesting and much more complex, even scientifically. Leave aside the fact that order is not an illusion, and if it were (or if the order were not somehow knowable), science could not be undertaken. Monod is interested in contingency and chance as an alternative to God. To explain things as "by chance" means for Monod that God and purpose and

2. H. Fries, "Myth," in *Encyclopedia of Theology: The Concise Sacramentum Mundi,* ed. K. Rahner (New York: Seabury Press, 1975), pp. 1011-12; cited by Daniel P. Sulmasy, "Every *Ethos* Implies a *Mythos:* Faith and Bioethics," in *Notes from a Narrow Ridge: Religion and Bioethics,* ed. Dena S. Davis and Laurie Zoloth (Hagerstown, MD: University Publishing Group, 1999), p. 230.

myth are — and must be — debunked by anyone who would adopt a scientific attitude. But Monod does not escape myth! Instead he adopts the myth of the casino: deep down the world is as it is as a result of a Monte Carlo game.[3] As Mary Midgley observed in response to Monod, however, that myth will not wash. Casinos are "not chancy things at all but highly purposive human artifacts, devices to produce a peculiar arrangement that is never normally found in nature — namely a calculated disorder which can baffle prediction."[4] Monod's myth is a bad myth, and a dangerous one. It renders the world, as he admits, "chillingly value free."[5] Scientific knowledge, according to Monod, provides the only source of value. It is an odd and presumptuous claim, especially given the fact that Monod sometimes also claims that science is just about establishing "facts." The point is not that we should treat God as a scientific hypothesis; the point is simply that myth is inescapable, even for those who would debunk myths. The point is not to throw suspicion on the sciences; the point is rather that science needs a context that science itself cannot provide, a context provided by something akin to myth.

The problem is not that there are myths; the problem is that there are bad myths. Monod may serve as an illustration not only of the fact that myth is inescapable but also of the fact that some myths are better than others. Myths, of course, are frequently unexamined and unquestioned. Indeed, they can so order our thoughts that they seem unquestionable.

---

3. Jacques Monod, *Chance and Necessity,* trans. Austryn Wainhouse (London and Glasgow: Collins, Fount, 1977), p. 137.

4. Mary Midgley, *Science as Salvation: A Modern Myth and Its Meaning* (London and New York: Routledge, 1992), p. 42.

5. The quote is from Midgley, p. 38. For Monod's claims about science as moral guide see *Chance and Necessity,* pp. 164-65.

Still, there are good reasons to question Monod's myth of the casino. And there are surely good reasons — both reasons of science and reasons of humanity — to doubt the Nazi myth or the Marxist account of "dialectical materialism." Some myths finally will not wash. And some of the myths that have formed our minds about nature and about altering it are, I think, stories ripe for doubt.

Consider briefly the following: "the gene myth," the myth of "the Baconian project," the myth of the project of liberal society, the myth of capitalism, the dominant social matrix produced by the constellation of these last three myths, and the myth of Romanticism.

1. The Gene Myth

Consider, first, what Ted Peters and others have called "the gene myth."[6] Peters identifies the gene myth with the slogan, "It's all in the genes."[7] A moment's reflection may be sufficient to identify and dismiss "the gene myth" as another form of reductionism, but myths, as we said, frequently go unexamined. There have been various forms of reductionism, of course, but they all have this in common, that they reduce the whole of nature and/or human nature to one part of it. The slogans of reductionism are always "It's all in the . . . X" and nature and/or human nature "is nothing but . . . X." To understand X is presumably to understand nature and/or human nature, and to control X is presumably to

6. Ted Peters, *Playing God? Genetic Determinism and Human Freedom* (New York: Routledge, 1997), pp. xiii, 5, following Ruth Hubbard and Elijah Wald, *Exploding the Gene Myth* (Boston: Beacon Press, 1993).

7. Peters, *Playing God?,* p. xiii.

control nature and/or human nature. Idealistic forms of reductionism take X to be the mind or ideas of the mind. Scientific forms of reductionism take X to be some item susceptible to a scientific explanation and to technological control. Various parts of the whole have been favored at various times, from the atom to the gene, but the most current form of reductionism is genetic reductionism, or "the gene myth." Mark the rhetoric that frequently surrounds the study of the human genome.

When in 1953 James Watson and Francis Crick discovered the structure of DNA,[8] the now familiar "double helix," they celebrated their discovery in a pub near their lab, where Crick announced to those gathered that they had just discovered "the secret of life."[9] That sort of rhetoric is commonplace in pubs, I suppose, but it was to grow commonplace also in the descriptions of the genome. It was the "Bible" for life, the "Book of Man," "the Holy Grail."[10]

Walter Gilbert, a Nobel laureate in genetics, made the plausible prediction that we will each one day have a CD containing a map of our individual genetic code. But he went on to make the foolish suggestion that we could hold up that CD and say, "This is me."[11] Such a future (along with such rheto-

8. Their "discovery" was itself dependent upon the work of Rosalind Franklin and Maurice Wilkins. For a history of genetics, see Horace Freeland Judson, *The Eighth Day of Creation* (New York: Simon & Schuster, 1979) , and the autobiographical account of James D. Watson, *The Double Helix* (New York: Atheneum, 1968).

9. Watson, *The Double Helix*, p. 126.

10. Dorothy Nelkin and M. Susan Lindee, *The DNA Mystique: The Gene as a Cultural Icon* (New York: W. H. Freeman, 1995).

11. Walter Gilbert, "A Vision of the Grail," in Daniel Kevles and Leroy Hood, eds., *The Code of Codes: Scientific and Social Issues in the Human Genome Project* (Cambridge, MA: Harvard University Press, 1992), p. 96.

ric) we must resist and reject. The human person may not be reduced to her genes. The ability to map and sequence the genes does not give us what Gilbert hoped for, "the ultimate answer to the [ancient] commandment 'know thyself.'"[12] Indeed, not even the body may be reduced to genes; a genotype is not to be confused with a phenotype.[13] Persons and bodies have histories, not just genetic fates. No living thing may be reduced to its genes; each living thing stands in a symbiotic relationship to other things, and that relationship will affect the expression (and the utility) of genes. Good science acknowledges and, indeed, demonstrates the folly of "the gene myth." The media, however, and the general public seem less sober-minded, captivated by what Dorothy Nelkin and Susan Lindee call "the DNA mystique."

But what is it that the Human Genome Project mapped? Not the human person. Not the human body. Not even that thing called "the human genome." There is no such *thing* as "*the* human genome." The Human Genome Project itself reminded us that genes differ from person to person. The aim of the project was to publish the average or "consensus" sequence of 200 different people. But that provided a map neither of everyone nor of anyone. Does "*the* human genome" have blood group A? or B? or AB? or O? We know where to look on chromosome 9 for a marker for blood type, but if we look carefully, we will not see the blood type of "*the* human genome." We will see that "Variation is an inherent and integral part of the human — or indeed any — ge-

12. Jean Bethke Elshtain, *Who Are We? Critical Reflections and Hopeful Possibilities* (Grand Rapids: Eerdmans, 2000), p. 90, citing Gilbert.

13. See James F. Keenan, SJ, "Genetic Research and the Elusive Body," in Lisa Sowle Cahill and Margaret A. Farley, eds., *Embodiment, Morality, and Medicine* (Dordrecht: Kluwer, 1995), pp. 59-73, p. 63.

nome."[14] The genome project might teach us not genetic reductionism but the importance of biodiversity.

Or, again: What is it that the Human Genome Project maps? It is easy to get the impression that what it really locates are diseases. Open a catalogue on the human genome and you are confronted with a list of diseases. Open a newspaper and you are confronted with a series of headlines: "New gene for mental illness." "Gene for kidney cancer isolated." "A new Alzheimer's gene." "Yet," as Matt Ridley says,[15]

> to define genes by the diseases they cause is about as absurd as defining organs of the body by the diseases they get; livers are there to cause cirrhosis, hearts to cause heart attacks and brains to cause strokes. It is a measure, not of our knowledge but of our ignorance that this is the way the genome catalogues read. It is literally true that the only thing we know about some genes is that their malfunction causes a particular disease. This is a pitifully small thing to know about a gene, and a terribly misleading one.

If this is not enough to lower the rhetoric and to dispel genetic reductionism, consider the folly of the genetic determinism that accompanies such reductionism. Its folly is displayed, I think, in the contradiction such determinism almost always invokes. On the one hand, it denies human freedom, insisting that human beings are totally determined by their "nature," that is to say, their DNA. On the other hand, it insists that hu-

---

14. Matt Ridley, *Genome: The Autobiography of the Species* (New York: HarperCollins, 1999), p. 145.
15. Ridley, *Genome,* pp. 54-55.

man beings are free, free indeed to alter and control their DNA, their own "nature," and their evolutionary future.[16]

That the gene has become "a cultural icon, a symbol, almost a magical force" has been well displayed by Dorothy Nelkin and M. Susan Lindee in *The DNA Mystique: The Gene as a Cultural Icon*. The rhetoric about the gene sustains a "genetic essentialism" that "reduces the self to a molecular entity, equating human beings, in all their social, historical, and moral complexity, with their genes."[17]

16. See Peters, *Playing God?*, p. xiii:

> The growing myth of genetic determinism blows first in one direction: if we are programmed totally by our DNA, then what we think is human freedom is in fact a delusion. Then the myth blows the opposite way: if we can apply our best engineering technology to DNA, then we can gain control over nature and guide our own evolutionary future. The genes determine the future; we want to determine the genes.

17. Nelkin and Lindee, *The DNA Mystique*, p. 2. To give one further example of genetic reductionism, consider "the God gene." We are accustomed to triumphal reports about the discovery of a gene for this or that or the other thing — for Huntington's, for obesity, for violence, for altruism, and the list goes on. But the claim to have discovered "the God Gene" (Dean Hamer, *The God Gene: How Faith Is Hardwired into Our Genes*) was still a little shocking. How might Christians respond to such a claim?

We might first observe that genetics itself has taught us to appreciate the complexity of genetic inheritance. To be sure, the formula of one gene for one disease does sometimes work. There is, for example, a location on chromosome 4 that is linked to Huntington's disease. But even in that case, the variation in the expression of the genetic mutation is large, and some people with the mutation are unaffected. And typically things are even more complicated. Scientists themselves call attention to the complex interplay of genes with each other and with social and environmental factors. It is appropriate to be a little suspicious of the claim that "faith is hardwired" into us by the presence of cytosine at a particular location in the gene VMAT2. But leaving aside that particular claim, how should peo-

The gene myth may pretend to wisdom, as if the human genome were the "secret of life" or the "code of codes" or the "map of human life," but we should reject this way of thinking about and talking about nature and about human nature. We should reject genetic reductionism. Genetic reductionism provides one way to read the map of the human genome — as if it were necessary and sufficient for understanding human nature and for gaining the wisdom to alter it. But that is the way of folly, not wisdom.

When we reject scientific reductionism, we do not reject the sciences. And when we reject genetic reductionism, we do not reject the study of genetics. And when we refuse the reduction of our nature to our genes, we should not deny their significance or claim simple transcendence over them. Nor do we reject out of hand the power to alter the genes. Rather, we reject the claim that the map of the human genome is suf-

---

ple of faith respond to efforts to discover a gene for human spirituality, to locate human spirituality within our genetic endowment? Without fear but not without suspicion. We may respond without fear because the idea that we are spiritual beings "by nature" is hardly a new idea, and our "nature" surely includes our genome even if it cannot be reduced to it. If God is the maker of heaven and earth — and of the human genome — then one might welcome the claim that our genetic endowment can support a *sensus divinitatis.* In the little concordance of A's, C's, G's, and T's there is an entry for spirituality. Good! Worship goes with the grain of our nature, not against it. But the genetically normal is not to be confused with the morally and spiritually normative. And the rhetoric frequently surrounding such research should make us a little suspicious. There are dangers of genetic reductionism and determinism in that rhetoric when it invites us to read the map of the human genome as if it were sufficient for understanding human life. We should reject that way of thinking about and talking about both the human genome and about human spirituality. Christian spirituality is formed and informed by a particular history and community, not simply "hardwired" by cytosine in VMAT2.

ficient to locate its own significance. We acknowledge, that is, the necessity of some other map or maps of nature and human nature, some other ways to locate and to orient ourselves with respect to the knowledge of nature and the power over nature that the sciences provide, some other myth. There is no great wisdom in rejecting the gene myth, but there is no hope for wisdom unless we do.

2. The Baconian Myth

Consider also the myth invoked by what has been aptly named "the Baconian project."[18] The Baconian project locates the study of nature as a "practical" science and orients it toward "the relief of human subjection to fate or necessity."[19] That sounds commendable enough, and it is surely commonplace enough in the modern world. But it invokes a myth that is ripe for doubt and invites us to folly.

It is not folly to distinguish the "practical" from the "speculative" (or theoretical) sciences. Aquinas had done that.

---

18. On the Baconian project see Gerald McKenny, *To Relieve the Human Condition: Bioethics, Technology, and the Body* (Albany: State University of New York Press, 1997). Francis Bacon himself, to be sure, intended his "great instauration" to be a form of obedience to God, as a restoration of humanity to the mastery of nature that was given with the creation but lost through the fall. See below on Bacon as an interpreter of Scripture. Indeed, he prays "that things human may not interfere with things divine, and that . . . there may arise in our minds no incredulity or darkness with regard to the divine mysteries" (Francis Bacon, *The New Organon and Other Writings,* ed. R. H. Anderson [Indianapolis: Bobbs-Merrill, 1960 (1620)], pp. 14-15). Bacon provided, however, no place on his map of knowledge for the knowledge of such mysteries.

19. McKenny, *To Relieve the Human Condition,* p. 22.

Aquinas, however, affirmed that all knowledge is "good."[20] Bacon, however, distinguished them in order to reject the "speculative" sciences as the mere "boyhood of knowledge" and as "barren of works."[21] Western culture has followed Bacon in exalting a particular form of knowledge, the knowledge for which it reserves the honorific term "science." In the classical account, theory (or the speculative sciences) provided the wisdom to use the practical sciences appropriately. In Bacon's account, where shall we look for wisdom?

The modern account may admit, as Bacon did, that for knowledge to be beneficial humanity must "perfect and govern it in charity,"[22] but science is "not self-sufficiently the source of that human quality that makes it beneficial."[23] Genetic research has not yet found a marker for charity. Moreover, the compassion or charity that responds viscerally to suffering will urge *us to do something* in response to suffering, but it will not tell us *what thing* to do. Given our Baconian confidence in the "practical" sciences, in technology, it is little wonder that the thing to do is to reach for the latest technique or the nearest tool in an effort to put an end to suffering. Our enthusiasm for technology, and for the art of altering nature as a response to suffering, has blinded us to the limits of technology. The Baconian account of knowledge simply arms compassion with artifice, not with wisdom. It trains compassion to eliminate suffering, not to bear it, not to share it. For the knowledge to "perfect and gov-

20. Aquinas, *Commentary on Aristotle's On the Soul* 1.3; cited in Hans Jonas, *The Phenomenon of Life: Toward a Philosophical Biology* (Boston: Beacon Press, 1966), p. 188.

21. Bacon, *The New Organon and Other Writings,* p. 8.

22. Bacon, *The New Organon and Other Writings,* p. 15.

23. Hans Jonas, *The Phenomenon of Life: Toward a Philosophical Biology* (New York: Dell, 1966), p. 195.

ern" human powers and for the wisdom to guide charity, science must call upon something else. But upon what? And how, in Bacon's account, can humanity have "knowledge" of it?[24]

The "practical" knowledge Bacon celebrated was sought in the confidence that it would render humanity "capable of overcoming the difficulties and obscurities of nature,"[25] able to subdue and overcome the vexations and miseries that nature brings, and "to endow the human family with new mercies."[26] Knowledge, in Bacon's view, is power over nature, and the myth is that mastery over nature inevitably brings human wellbeing in its train. That is a myth shared by much of Western culture. It is important once again to observe that many sober-minded scientists and engineers acknowledge the folly of such extravagant expectations of science and technology. Nevertheless, the *mythos* persists, establishing an *ethos* of confidence in technology to remedy our problems, including the problems created by technology.

The myth of the Baconian project sets humanity not only

24. Knowledge of that which transcends "use" — and transcends the "nature" known scientifically, even the "human nature" known scientifically — has no place in Bacon's account. The irony, of course, is that science does not tell us what to do with the great power it gives. It does not tell us what ends to seek or what limits to observe. It cannot tell us how to use these great powers without violating the material, including the human material, upon which they are used. At the end of the story, even as we continue to tell it, we know better. Human progress cannot be reduced to scientific progress. Every good doctor knows that knowing a patient cannot be reduced to scientific knowing. Indeed, if the complaints of some patients are to be credited, the scientific "view" can distort the vision of physicians and blind them to persons and to the body as "me." See also Michel Foucault's account of the "clinical gaze" in *The Birth of the Clinic: An Archaeology of Medical Perception* (New York: Vintage, 1973).

25. Bacon, *The New Organon and Other Writings,* p. 19.

26. Bacon, *The New Organon and Other Writings,* p. 29.

over nature but against it. The natural order and natural processes have no dignity of their own; their value is reduced to their utility to humanity. And nature does not serve humanity "naturally." Nature threatens to rule and to ruin humanity. The fault that runs through our world and through our lives must finally be located in nature. In the myth of the Baconian project, nature is the enemy. Nature may be — and must be — mastered. It may be — and must be — altered. In this myth technology becomes the faithful savior.

When we reject the myth of the Baconian project, we do not reject either the sciences or all of the technologies by which human beings intervene in natural processes to alter nature. We are the beneficiaries, after all, of the advances in medical science and technology that can be attributed to the Baconian project. And the science of ecology is important to any effort today to care for the creation. Rather, we reject the myth that has grown up around our scientific and technological powers, that nature is the enemy and that technology will deliver us from our finitude and mortality and to our flourishing. We reject the claim that science and technology need no larger vision, no "speculative knowledge," to guide and limit their powers to alter nature. Science and technology are not sufficient to locate their own significance. We acknowledge, that is, the necessity of some other *mythos,* some other map or maps of nature and human nature, some other ways to locate and to orient ourselves with respect to the knowledge and power that the sciences give.[27]

27. The ambitions of the Baconian project extend to human finitude itself, to human nature. It finds a natural expression in genetic enhancement. Because nature has no moral standing, because the nature we are is the nature we suffer from, if nature or humanity can be "enhanced," they should be. As Mark Hanson observed, the Baconian project will find it in-

Promethean pride is at work in the effort to eliminate our anxiety by eliminating the insecurity that attends our finitude. The Baconian confidence that technology inevitably brings human wellbeing in its train is a myth ripe for doubt. The Baconian project is a powerful — but foolish — myth to map nature, to locate us and to orient us within it. We must look for wisdom elsewhere.

3. The Myth of the Project of Liberal Society

There is another myth familiar to the modern world in the project of liberal society, although it is seldom recognized as myth. Indeed, it would bracket myth, set it aside as anathema. But the myth here is that we can and should (in public, anyway) live without myth. The story is that we can and should do without stories.

The project of liberal society and its myth may be traced to the commendable effort of the Enlightenment to make peace in the midst of difference. In the midst of religious and moral diversity, the project of liberal society is to keep the peace.[28] That, too, is commendable enough, and it is surely commonplace enough in the modern (and postmodern)

---

creasingly difficult to think (or to make and preserve) a distinction between healing and enhancement. There is an irony here, however. The very success of enhancement technologies "serves to broaden the scope of conditions from which humans can be said to suffer" (Mark J. Hanson, "Indulging Anxiety: Human Enhancement from a Protestant Perspective," *Christian Bioethics* 5, no. 2 [August 1999]: 121-38, p. 125).

28. See the treatment of "the liberal convention" in Hans Reinders, *The Future of the Disabled in Liberal Society: An Ethical Analysis* (Notre Dame: University of Notre Dame Press, 2000), pp. 22-35.

world, but again there are problems with this myth when examined.

There is the obvious self-referential problem with the myth that we can do without myth, akin to the moral certainty that there can be no moral certainty. Set that problem aside for now. Because people disagree widely and deeply about their religious and moral convictions, a liberal society insists that we bracket those convictions, that we set aside the myths and stories by which people live, and that public moral discourse attend only to the requirement of the maximum freedom for each member of the society that is compatible with a like freedom for all others. A liberal society insists on respect for the autonomy of each person, demands the protection of individual rights, and attempts to guarantee a space for each one to act in ways that suit one's moral preferences as long as such actions do not violate the autonomy of another. Now, it is not folly to attempt to keep the peace in the midst of diversity. It is not folly to insist on respect for the moral integrity of each member of a diverse society. But the weakness of the project of liberal society is precisely its minimalism, and its folly is its failure (or its refusal) to acknowledge this minimalism.

Its minimalism shows up in a variety of ways. First, the liberal project tells us nothing about what goods to seek, only something about certain constraints to exercise in seeking them. Moreover, it is attentive to only one constraint: prohibiting any violation of another's freedom. Second, it reduces covenantal relationships (like the relationships between doctor and patient, husband and wife, parent and child) to matters of contract. Third, by its emphasis on the procedural question — the question "Who should decide?" — it pushes to the margins of public discourse the substantive moral questions of conduct and character, the questions "What should be decided?" and "What virtues should mark the one who decides?" Finally, and fundamentally, for the sake of our pluralism the liberal project requires of people who would engage in public discourse that they disown or disregard the particular moral communities and convictions that give them their moral identities and their moral passions. There is an irony here, of course. The irony of the requirement of moral minimalism for the sake of our pluralism is that it is suspicious of and inhospitable to difference. At its best, it is the discourse of those who, in spite of their differences, resolve to live together as peaceful strangers, but it can hardly nurture any other form of community than that of wary and spiteful strangers who want to be protected from one another.

Its moral minimalism does not make the liberal project wrong, but if its minimalism is not acknowledged, it can distort and subvert the moral life — and our relationship with nature. It is true, for example, that "non-consensual sex" is wrong — but there is more to say about a good sexual life, and if we deny that there is more to say, then we distort and subvert a good sexual life. Spouses frequently resort to the language of contract, to the "rights" and "duties" that belong to the contract — usually in the middle of an argument — and it is frequently good that they can invoke such language. But if that is the only language they have for their relationship, then they distort and subvert the covenant of marriage.

Pretending to bracket any fundamental view of nature or of human nature, the liberal project and its myth reduce nature to commodity and human nature to the capacities for agency. Advocates of "reproductive liberty," for example, like John Robertson in *Children of Choice,* sometimes dismiss "symbolic concerns" when considering assisted reproductive technologies (or technologies that alter "natural" procreation) because reasonable people disagree about their religious and moral convictions.[29] They offer instead a thin account of human life and parenting, a disembodied and individualistic account. Individuals are presented as pure subjects, isolated wills, over and over against nature, over and over against their own bodies, which are regarded as objects. So, the self is reduced to capacities for agency, and acts of begetting are reduced to physiology and matters of contract. The myth is that we can (and should) live without myth. But the account offered of our humanity and our begetting in such cases should not be regarded as less "symbolic" because it is so thin. We may succeed in making our accounts of begetting boring, but we will not succeed in making them nonsymbolic. Views of begetting along with views of nature and human nature always come with metaphysical baggage, are always accompanied by myth. The question is not which view is "symbolic" and which is not. The question is which symbolic view is wisdom and which is folly.

Consider the folly of commercial surrogacy. Surrogate mothers are sometimes alienated from the embodied experience of pregnancy and birth (and their bonding effects) by the contract and sometimes alienated from the contract by their embodied experience. Better yet, consider the bad faith of those who would contract with a surrogate mother. Because they regard *some* biological relationship with the child to be important, they encourage the surrogate to regard *her* biological relationship with the child as morally trivial.

---

29. John A. Robertson, *Children of Choice: Freedom and the New Reproductive Technologies* (Princeton: Princeton University Press, 1994). See the review of Robertson's work in Gilbert Meilaender, *Body, Soul, and Bioethics* (Notre Dame: University of Notre Dame Press, 1995), pp. 61-88.

Or consider the apparent incoherence of the project of liberal society with regard to disabled persons. As Hans Reinders says,[30]

> On the one hand, it supports full citizenship for the disabled in order to realize their inclusion in society. This commitment is justified by one of the pillars of liberal morality, e.g., the right to equal opportunity. On the other hand, it is committed to the right to reproductive freedom that includes the freedom to prevent a child with a disability from being born. It is not easy to see how public morality in liberal society can keep the balance between both of these commitments.

Finally, however, the folly of the myth of liberal society is displayed in the pretense that "maximizing freedom" or "increasing options" is always morally innocent. "Maximizing freedom," however, can ironically increase our bondage. What is introduced as a way to increase our options can become socially enforced. The point can easily be illustrated with technology. New technologies are frequently introduced as ways to increase our options, as ways to maximize our freedom, but they can become socially enforced. The automobile was introduced as an option, as an alternative to the horse, but it is now socially enforced. The horse remains, I suppose, a "recreational vehicle," but don't try to ride one home on the interstate! The technology that surrounds our dying was introduced to give doctors and patients options in the face of disease and death, but such "options" have become socially enforced; at least one sometimes still hears, "We have no

30. Reinders, *The Future of the Disabled*, p. 65. See also pp. 77-78.

choice!" And the technology that may come to surround birth, including pre-natal diagnosis, for example, may come to be socially enforced. "What? You knew you were at risk for bearing a child with XYZ (or, I suppose, XYY), and you did nothing about it? And now you expect help with this child?" Now, it is possible, of course, to claim that cars and CPR and pre-natal diagnosis are the path of progress, but then the argument has shifted from the celebration of options and the maximizing of freedom to something else, to the meaning of progress. And that argument, of course, requires more substantive moral convictions than the liberal project is prepared to invoke; it requires something like a myth. If the myth is that technological progress is always human and moral progress, then the problem is resolved, of course, but that Baconian myth is, as we have seen, ripe for doubt.

Moreover, even if a particular option does not become socially enforced, simply providing the option, simply "maximizing freedom" by giving social legitimization to certain choices, can and does affect the determinate features of our life and our common life. Our choices, even to regard certain things as choices, form selves, and our social choices, even to increase options, form our common life. Consider, for example, the life of a night clerk at the convenience store.[31] One determinate feature of her existence is frequently identified on the front door: "The night clerk cannot open the safe." To maximize the freedom of this night clerk, one might give her the option of opening the safe. But to increase her options in this way would change the determinate features of her life, and not happily — or innocently: not happily because, given

31. J. David Velleman, "Against the Right to Die," *The Journal of Medicine and Philosophy* 17 (December 1992): 665-81, p. 671.

the vulnerability of a night clerk, to change the determinate features of her life in that way would lessen her security; and not innocently because, under cover of maximizing freedom, we would be regarding the vulnerability of others as a matter of moral indifference.

Notice also that choices to increase options can sometimes eliminate options.[32] We have all had the experience of the unwelcome invitation. The invitation is presented as an option, of course. But by increasing our options, the invitation effectively eliminated what we may suddenly recognize as the option we would have preferred, the option we had a moment ago but have no longer, the option of *both* not spending more time with the person who made the invitation *and* not having to think of a polite explanation or excuse. The invitation, by increasing our options, maximizing our freedom, has put us in a bind and eliminated the option we wish we still had. When, under cover of maximizing freedom, we offer the option of physician-assisted suicide, we eliminate the option of staying alive without having to justify one's existence to anyone. And when, under cover of reproductive liberty, we offer the option of preventing birth defects by preventing the births of defectives, we eliminate the option of having and caring for a child without having to justify the child's existence to anyone. Maximizing freedom should not be regarded as a sufficient justification for a change in social practices, especially if they leave the weak still more vulnerable.

Finally, by its myopic attention to capacities for agency, it leaves nature still more vulnerable. Care and respect are made contingent upon the possession of some capacities analogous to the choice-making capacities of adult human

32. Velleman, "Against the Right to Die," p. 672.

beings. The obligation to care for nature is reduced to an obligation to respect the persons whose interests may be at stake in the treatment of an animal or a piece of land or the ecology.

When we reject the myth of the project of liberal society, we do not reject the moral significance of freedom. Freedom is a great good, the prerequisite for the moral life, but it is not sufficient. The minimalism to which we have called attention does not mark freedom as insignificant, but if its insufficiency is not acknowledged, the myopic emphasis on freedom can distort and subvert the moral life. Rather, we reject the myth that we can do without myth, the story that we can do without story, the confidence that if we simply maximize freedom, all will be well. The confidence that maximizing freedom is always morally unobjectionable is a creed ripe for doubt. The myth of the project of liberal society is a powerful — but foolish — map to locate ourselves within and to orient ourselves to nature and human nature. We must look for wisdom elsewhere.

4. The Myth of the Project of Capitalism

There is another myth deep in our culture, the myth of the capitalist project. It, too, was on display in the Human Genome Project. It became increasingly clear that the growth in genetic knowledge and power were connected to the financial incentives that fueled it. The project of capitalism transformed scientific knowledge into a marketable commodity.[33]

33. Jean-François Lyotard, *The Postmodern Condition: A Report on Knowledge* (Manchester: Manchester University Press, 1992), pp. 4-5:

The relationship of the suppliers and users of knowledge to the knowledge they supply and use is now tending, and will increasingly tend, to assume

Those at the forefront of investment in genetics — the United States, the European nations, and Japan — expect lucrative returns in commercial applications by their biotechnology industries.[34] At the beginning of the international research effort it was cost-effectiveness that was invoked to justify the coordinated and collaborative effort.[35] Subsequently, as particular diseases were identified with particular sequences, in order to assure investment in research and product development, the commercial interests of the biotechnology companies led to the patenting of gene se-

---

the form already taken by the relationship of commodity producers and consumers to the commodities they produce and consume — that is, the form of value. Knowledge is and will be produced in order to be sold; it is and will be consumed in order to be valorized in a new production. In both cases the goal is exchange.

I owe this citation to Julie Clague, "Genetic Knowledge as a Commodity: The Human Genome Project, Markets and Consumers," in Maureen Junker-Kenny and Lisa Sowle Cahill, eds., *The Ethics of Genetic Engineering* (*Concilium* 2 [1998]; London: SCM Press, 1998), pp. 3-12, p. 6.

34. Not to mention returns in the form of political power. Again see Clague, p. 6, still citing Lyotard, p. 5:

Knowledge in the form of an informational commodity indispensable to productive power is already, and will continue to be, a major — perhaps *the* major — stake in the worldwide competition for power. It is conceivable that the nation-states will one day fight for control of information, just as they battled in the past for control over territory, and afterwards for control of access to and exploitation of raw materials and cheap labour. A new field is opened for industrial and commercial strategies on the one hand, and political and military strategies on the other.

35. Robert Mullan Cook-Deegan, "Genome Mapping and Sequencing," in Warren Reich, ed., *Encyclopedia of Bioethics,* rev. ed. (New York: Macmillan, 1995), pp. 1011-20, 1014-15. See also Karen Lebacqz, "Fair Shares: Is the Genome Project Just?" in Ted Peters, ed., *Genetics: Issues of Social Justice* (Cleveland: Pilgrim Press, 1998), pp. 82-107.

quences.[36] Collaboration and cooperation gave way to competition and secrecy because the market demanded it.

The medical advances promised by the growth in genetic science in technology are tied to successful (i.e., commercially successful) product development by biotechnology companies. Social benefits depend upon the market, and the medical goals are intimately related to commercial goals. The beneficiaries of the Human Genome Project, both economically and medically, will very likely live in the developed nations, and indeed they will very likely be among the relatively well off within those populations. It is hardly accidental that the most studied gene is the cystic fibrosis gene; 1 in 25 northern Europeans carry it.[37]

Perhaps we are to believe the myth of the capitalist project, that some "invisible hand" will guide the market toward not only efficiency but also toward global equity. Perhaps we are to believe that, if we simply leave the market free from interference, at least some benefits will "trickle down" to the poor and economically powerless. But this is a creed ripe for doubt. What we have seen so far does not bode well for global justice — or for nature.

To be sure, the application of genetic engineering to agriculture has increased agricultural production. The perennial problems of weeds and pests have been addressed by modifying the genome of plants like corn and soybeans.[38] Monsanto,

36. See Stephen Sherry, "The Incentive of Patents," in John F. Kilner, Rebecca D. Pentz, and Frank E. Young, eds., *Genetic Ethics: Do the Ends Justify the Genes?* (Grand Rapids: Eerdmans, 1997), pp. 113-23.

37. There is an obvious connection between the liberal project and the project of capitalism. New technological developments are introduced as ways to increase choice for consumers.

38. See Daniel G. Deffenbaugh, *Learning the Language of the Fields:*

for example, which produces "Roundup," has created a genetically modified seed that it calls "Roundup Ready." These crops can withstand "Roundup," which can then be used liberally to eliminate the weeds. But using Roundup liberally in one field planted with "Roundup Ready" seed may result in the pesticide being carried into a neighbor's field planted with seed that does not carry the genetic protection. The neighbor will then lose part of his crop to the pesticide and have little choice other than adopting "Roundup Ready" for the next planting.

Monsanto also has a patent on a genetic modification of plants that introduces the bacterium *Bacillus thuringiensis* into its cotton, corn, and potato seeds. The bacterium is an effective remedy against the larvae of certain pests who eat the plants, ingesting the bacteria. It has been used effectively by organic farmers, but when it is used on a large scale, it can promise only a short-term solution, and it threatens disaster over the longer term. *Bacillus thuringiensis* kills most but not all of the pests, and the ones it does not kill, the ones that have a genetic resistance to the effects of the bacterium, will go on reproducing, and its larvae will have plenty of cropland on which to feed and grow to reproduce. The result might be not control of the pest but the creation of a strain of pest resistant to such control.

One other genetic alteration of plants under development by the big agri-chemical firms would modify plants so that their seed is sterile until treated with an agent, a catalyst sold, of course, by the same agri-chemical company. Perhaps we are to believe the myth of the capitalist project, that some "invisible hand" will guide the market not only toward efficiency

Tilling and Keeping as Christian Vocation (Cambridge, MA: Cowley, 2006), pp. 93-98.

and global equity but also toward biodiversity and sustainability. But this is a creed ripe for doubt. What we have seen so far does not bode well for the environment, for the small farmer, or for our food supply.[39] What we have seen so far looks like a single-minded pursuit of profit, without attention to the other goods of a political economy.

There is another danger in the myth of the project of capitalism. It is the hold capitalism has not only on giant corporations but on us. Jim Wallis reports seeing a bumper sticker, "I Shop, Therefore I Am."[40] We have become a culture of consumers, and the more conspicuous the consumption, the better. We measure our lives by our toys, our worth by our "abundance of possessions" (Luke 12:15). This culture of consumerism distorts not only our self-concept but also our relationships with others and our relationship with nature. Everything becomes a marketable commodity. We know better, of course. At least we should know better. After all, we have rejected a market in human persons; we no longer have a slave market. We have prohibited a market regarding criminal justices; no one wants the verdicts of judge or jury to be bought and sold. Some things are not to be commodified or commercialized.[41] The point is obvious enough. But while we may see

39. On the environment see, for example, the website of the Action Group on Erosion, Technology, and Concentration, www.etcgroup.org. On the effects of corporate agriculture on the environment, on the small farmer, and on our culture see, for example, Wendell Berry, *The Unsettling of America: Culture and Agriculture* (San Francisco: Sierra Club, 1977) or almost any of his other books. On our food see, for example, Marc Lappé and Britt Bailey, *Against the Grain: Biotechnology and the Corporate Takeover of Your Food* (Monroe, ME: Common Courage Press, 1998).

40. Jim Wallis, *The Soul of Politics: Beyond "Religious Right" and "Secular Left"* (San Diego: Harcourt, Brace & Company, 1995), p. 151.

41. Michael Walzer calls these points at which we have limited the

the wisdom of blocking commercial exchange in some matters, like babies, and in allowing it in others, like six-penny nails, there are a host of things that may be placed on a market, but should never be reduced to mere vendible commodity. A home may be bought and sold, but it is not just a commodity. And land may be bought and sold, but it is not just "real estate." To reduce these things to commodities distorts the thing itself and our relationship to it. We may well worry a little that it is not just scientific knowledge that the project of capitalism transforms into a marketable commodity.

When we reject the myth of the project of capitalism, we do not reject the marketplace. We do not deny that the market is a good instrument for distributing many good things or for rewarding much good work. We do not claim that commerce is immoral or that markets are evil. But we reject the myth of the invisible hand that provides for the poor and protects the powerless, including the powerless environment. And we reject the reduction of everything to a marketable commodity. We reject the notion that everything has its price. There must be some other, some better, story to orient us toward both ourselves and others, toward homes and lands, toward nature. The myth of the project of capitalism is a powerful — but foolish — map to locate the significance of nature and the goods and limits for altering it. We must look for wisdom — and for justice — elsewhere.

---

sphere of the market "blocked exchanges," and he regards these limits on the sphere of the market as no less important to justice than "blocked uses of power," or the limits on the sphere of the state. Michael Walzer, *Spheres of Justice: A Defense of Pluralism and Equality* (New York: Basic Books, 1983), pp. 88-102.

5. The "Dominant Social Matrix"

The myth of the Baconian project, the myth of the project of liberal society, and the myth of the project of capitalism conspire together to form what Max Oelschlaeger has called the "dominant social matrix"[42] and what W. Harry Jellema might have called "the Modern Mind." Oelschlaeger identified the "dominant social matrix" with the following six items:

1. Nature has instrumental (anthropocentric) value only; biocentric values, such as the preservation of endangered species, are meaningless.
2. Short-term economic interests override long-term issues like intergenerational equity; future generations will be able to fend for themselves.
3. If environmental risks caused by habitat modification, consumption of resources, and the emission of pollution are economically beneficial (as measured monetarily), then they are acceptable.
4. Environmental risk poses no limits to growth, just problems that require engineered solutions. . . .
5. The strategy of managing planet Earth is feasible; through biotechnology and other sciences, humankind will ultimately be able to control all biophysical processes on the planet.
6. The politics of interest is sufficient to guarantee that the best available technology to restore habitat, devise resource substitutions, and control pollution will be employed.

---

42. Max Oelschlaeger, *Caring for Creation: An Ecumenical Approach to the Environmental Crisis* (New Haven: Yale University Press, 1994), p. 54.

The myth of the Baconian project echoes in the first, fourth, and fifth of the items identified by Oelschlaeger; the myth of the project of capitalism echoes in the second and third items; and the myth of the project of liberal society echoes in the sixth item.

Oelschlaeger effectively argued that the religious communities and their great narratives provide the best hope to challenge and reform "the dominant social matrix" and to help form a culture committed to "caring for creation."[43] But he admitted that the problem is complicated by what we have called the myth of the liberal project and by the hold that it evidently has also on members of religious communities. To quote him, "Although 90 percent of us have a religious affiliation, most of us apparently think of our religion as a private matter with little or no relevance to public issues."[44]

We may take our cue from Oelschlaeger to look for wisdom in the Christian tradition, in its "alternative story," the Bible. To quote him again, "the biblical tradition undergirds the largest (most extensive) and most effective community of memory operating in American society, a legitimating narrative that remains unencumbered by the modern story."[45] "Unencumbered" it is not, but the biblical narrative is nevertheless the best place to look for wisdom. Remember! Before we turn to Scripture and its wisdom about nature and altering it, however, there is one more myth that we should briefly examine.

---

43. That is the thesis of the book. See especially pp. 75-83. "Religion is the most likely way that Americans can move themselves to care for the Creation" (p. 75).

44. Oelschlaeger, *Caring for Creation,* p. 54.

45. Oelschlaeger, *Caring for Creation,* p. 83.

6. The Myth of Romanticism

The Romantic movement was a reaction to the Enlightenment's emphasis on unqualified reason and its confidence in science as a way to manage nature. It emphasized feelings and the imagination, and it rejected the image of nature as mechanism that had grown up with the scientific revolution. If Rousseau first uttered the slogan, "Back to Nature," the Romantics made it popular. The universe was not mechanical but organic, one living world spirit. The ways of God and the ways of nature were thought to be the same ways, and the aboriginal peoples were thought to be more in tune with those ways. The natural and the spiritual were expressions of the same Absolute spirit, and the one living world spirit could be sought either in nature or within. The myth was the old apotheosis of nature: "It's not nice to fool with Mother Nature."

Theoretically nature was to be seen as a whole, but Romanticism was largely an urban movement, and "nature" usually meant the countryside as opposed to the city, especially among its poets. Wordsworth congratulated Coleridge, for example, on the fact that, although he had been "reared in the great city," he had "long desired to serve in Nature's temple."[46] "Nature" stood in contrast to the city and to all that was made by humans. It meant green landscapes in a swirling mist. It nurtured, of course, a worthy affection for the natural environment, for wilderness and for ponds like one named Walden, and it provided an important challenge to the manipulative attitude toward nature. But the apotheosis of Nature was a creed that could not abide the city, and a creed that the city could not

46. *Prelude,* II, 452-63, cited by C. S. Lewis, *Studies in Words,* 2nd ed. (Cambridge: Cambridge University Press, 1967), p. 72.

abide, however attractive it may have been to discontented city-dwellers. However much Romanticism emphasized the one world spirit, for the sake of its own survival it accepted a compartmentalization of life. There was the city, where nature was used and altered, and there was wilderness where Nature's altar stood. There was a compartment for urban life and for measuring and manipulating nature, and there was a different place, wilderness, for awe and reverence before Nature. Of course, the city's grasp — along with the dominant social matrix — would eventually reach into the wilderness.

Such compartmentalization was a high price to pay, but it succeeded in preserving the Romantic myth. It still faintly echoes in the pipe-smoking old professor who puts on his mail-order hiking boots, drives his car out of the city a little ways to a little gravel path "untouched by the hand of man," and then, pausing on the path to admire "nature," exclaims that human beings should leave "nature" alone and unaltered. We are all tempted from time to time to this sort of compartmentalization, to being "double-minded," not to say hypocritical in our concern for nature. It is partly to resist such compartmentalization that the same pipe-smoking old professor insists on both attending to nature and altering it.

The Romantic myth — and the compartmentalization it accepted — echoed less ridiculously in the creation of a "forever wild" Adirondack forest preserve, Yellowstone (the first of the National Parks), and other "nature preserves" and wilderness areas, while cities and the reach of technology and the grasp of the dominant social matrix continued to grow. There is in such compartmentalization still sometimes an apotheosis of Nature, but the myth is sometimes content with a "god of the gaps," a god of those gaps where human alteration has not yet reached.

[42]

But the Romantic myth echoes also and most vigorously in "deep ecology." The work of Gary Snyder, sometimes called the poet laureate of deep ecology, is illustrative. His *Turtle Island* evoked a sense of a living and sacred "nature," a feminine and nurturing divinity. Those ancient people who lived in accord with nature, in tune with its rhythms, are celebrated as "sinking deeper and deeper in earth / up to your hips in Gods."[47] The compartmentalization remains, however, and human beings inevitably return to society, to the city. Nevertheless, Snyder hopes desperately that inspired by a sense of the sacred born again in the wilderness they will "see all the land about us, agricultural, suburban, urban, as part of the same territory — never totally ruined, never completely unnatural. It can be restored, and humans could live in considerable numbers on much of it."[48]

Less poetically but more provocatively J. Baird Callicott, another deep ecologist, evidently also wants to retrieve the ancient days when human life was lived in tune with nature and when the ways of nature were regarded as the ways of God.

> Rather than imposing our alienation from nature and natural processes and cycles of life on other animals, we human beings should reaffirm our participation in nature by accepting life as it is given without a sugar coating. Instead of imposing artificial legalities, rights, and so on on nature, we might take the opposite course and accept and affirm natural biological laws, principles,

47. Gary Snyder, *Turtle Island* (New York: New Directions, 1974), p. 3.
48. Gary Snyder, *The Practice of the Wild* (San Francisco: North Point Press, 1990), p. 94, cited by Oelschlaeger, p. 181.

and limitations in the human, personal, and social spheres. Such appears to have been the posture toward life of tribal peoples in the past. The chase was relished with its dangers, rigors, and hardships as well as its rewards: animal flesh was respectfully consumed; a tolerance for pain was cultivated; virtue and magnanimity were prized; lithic, floral, and faunal spirits were worshipped; population was routinely optimized by sexual contingency, abortion, infanticide, and stylized warfare; and other life forms, although certainly appropriated, were respected as fellow players in a magnificent and awesome, if not altogether idyllic, drama of life.[49]

Romanticism may still echo in such a proposal, but it sounds like a *reductio* designed to give predators an easy conscience. When the "survival of the fittest" is accepted not only as one of the "natural biological laws" but also as our own law, then pity the weak and powerless — including, if the personification be allowed, nature itself. Then nature, too, may desperately hope we find some other law, some other myth than the apotheosis of nature, some other wisdom.

So we would take up the invitation of Max Oelschlaeger to look to an "alternative story,"[50] the biblical story. To be sure,

---

49. J. Baird Callicott, "Animal Liberation: A Triangular Affair," *Environmental Ethics* 2 (Winter 1980): 334, cited in Robert N. Wennberg, *God, Humans, and Animals: An Invitation to Enlarge Our Moral Universe* (Grand Rapids: Eerdmans, 2003), p. 44.

50. Oelschlaeger, *Caring for Creation*, p. 76. Oelschlaeger gives an account of his own "conversion" from a bias against religion as underwriting environmental deterioration to a sense of the necessity of religious discourse and religious community if the "dominant social matrix" is to be successfully challenged.

the biblical story has been accused of being at the root of our "arrogance toward nature."[51] But by revisiting and retrieving the story of Scripture, we may provide an alternative to the myths we have so far considered, we may make a little progress in the formulation of a Christian "Mind" on nature and altering it, and we may be better prepared to meet and challenge the "dominant social matrix." If we take up the task of remembering the story well, we may be better prepared to discern what a faithful performance of the story would look like.

51. Lynn White, Jr., "The Historical Roots of Our Ecological Crisis," *Science* 155 (1967): 1203-7.

III

The Problem of Arrogance:
Reading Scripture Regarding Nature —
A Response to the Accusation of Lynn White, Jr.

In the first chapter we noted different notions of "nature." The little philological archaeology that we engaged in was of little help with the questions that interest us. The list of sixteen senses of "nature" that we left, still counting, only displayed that accounts of nature and altering it will always be embedded in larger visions, in myth.

Taking a cue from Aristotle's maxim, "Every *ethos* implies a *mythos*," we attempted in the second chapter to identify some of the myths that have shaped the modern Mind and that have shaped our relationship to nature and our attitude to altering it. We looked at "the gene myth," the myth of the Baconian project, the myth of the project of liberal society, the myth of the project of capitalism, and the Romantic myth. We saw, I hope, that these myths have shaped attitudes toward nature and toward altering it, and that they are creeds ripe for doubt.

I promised that we would turn next to the Christian "myth," to the story Scripture tells, for the story that should form the Christian Mind about these matters. But before we do, it is important to acknowledge that there are some problems when we turn to Scripture to look for wisdom concerning nature and altering it.

The first problem is simply the *silence* of Scripture. It is worth noting that the Hebrew language, in which, of course, the Old Testament was written, does not even have an equivalent term for *phusis,* or "nature." That does not mean, of course, that the Bible is silent about nature; it isn't. But it is silent about ecological science, about Lotka-Volterra equations, for example (which relate the capacity of an environment to support organisms, population size, time, and growth).[1] And it is silent about global warming and suburban sprawl, and a host of other contemporary ecological concerns. It is also silent, of course, about many of the ways we alter nature, including, for example, technological interventions into the natural history of a disease, technologies to alter natural processes of procreation, technologies of genetic modification, and the list could go on.

The mention of genetic modification may remind us of a second problem, the *strangeness* of Scripture. Consider, for example, the strange story of Jacob's success as a herdsman. After Jacob had been promised by Laban all the speckled goats (and Laban had removed all the speckled goats from the flock), Jacob cut the limbs of trees to expose speckles of white

1. Holmes Rolston III, "The Bible and Ecology," *Interpretation* 50, no. 1 (January 1996): 16-26, p. 17. He also observes that, even if Abraham and Lot did not have a scientific formula, they knew that the pastures they had been using could not support their flocks and herds, and so they separated (Gen. 13:3-11).

beneath the bark. Then he set the limbs where the goats would drink and breed. When the animals gave birth, the new goats were speckled like the limbs, and Jacob's flock increased (Gen. 30:31-39). That's a strange world of animal husbandry. Today a geneticist would probably simply tell Jacob to hope that many of Laban's goats were hetero-zy-goats. The joke is bad, but the point, I hope, is clear. The science and technology of the world of Scripture are quite different from our science and technology, and the world of Scripture can sometimes seem quite strange and alien to contemporary readers.

There is a third problem: the *diversity* of Scripture, also on this issue. The psalmist may celebrate nature for the praise it gives to God (e.g., Ps. 19), but Job 28 celebrates the technology that enables human beings to find and make precious metals (even if wisdom remains hidden from them and inaccessible to their ingenuity). Isaiah 11:6 envisions a future in which the wolf and the lamb will lie down together peaceably, while Ezekiel 34:25 envisions a future in which predatory animals are banished from the land.

And there is the problem of the *difficulty* of Scripture. It is by no means easy to decide, for example, exactly what Genesis 1 means by *rada* (Gen. 1:26, 28; NRSV: "have dominion") and *kabash* (Gen. 1:28; NRSV: "subdue").

But by far the biggest problem, here as in so many other areas of moral reflection, is not a problem with Scripture but a problem with us as readers of Scripture. The problem is our *interpretative arrogance,* our readiness to read Scripture in self-serving defense of our own righteousness and of the projects that are dear to us, rather than to read Scripture "over against" ourselves. Such interpretative arrogance has frequently led to the abuse of Scripture — and to the abuse of persons, usually marginalized and powerless persons, by means of the abuse of Scripture.

In the history of Christian deliberations about nature and about altering it, and in the history of Christian reading and performance of the biblical story with respect to nature, there has also frequently been such interpretative arrogance. And it has led both to the abuse of Scripture and to the abuse of nature as warranted by an abused Scripture. It is the abuse of Scripture and the interpretative arrogance of some readers of Scripture that has led to arrogance toward nature, not Scripture itself.

A Response to Lynn White, Jr.

That last paragraph forms my response to the widely read — and widely anthologized — essay by Lynn White, Jr., "The Historical Roots of Our Ecological Crisis."[2] In that essay White claimed that Christianity and its Scripture "bears a huge burden of guilt for environmental deterioration." According to White, the story of creation and especially of God's gift of "dominion" to human beings (Gen. 1:26-28) were the roots of what he called "the orthodox Christian arrogance toward nature." The Genesis story, according to White, set human beings apart from nature, above nature; it advocated mastery over nature; and it suggested that the natural world exists simply and solely to serve human ends. "Our science and technology," he said, "have grown out of Christian attitudes toward man's relation to nature. . . . We are superior

2. Lynn White, Jr., "The Historical Roots of Our Ecological Crisis," *Science* 155 (1967): 1203-7.

to nature, contemptuous of it, willing to use it for our slightest whim. . . ."

Before we turn to Scripture for wisdom about nature and altering it, we had better think carefully about how to respond to that accusation. We must agree, I think, that there is a problem here, a problem that White quite properly identifies as an "arrogance toward nature" supported by certain biblical texts; but we may and must ask, I think, whether the problem is with Scripture or with the interpretative arrogance of some readers of Scripture. If the problem is with Scripture, then some other strategy than the one I have laid out for this little book would be required. If the problem is interpretative arrogance, then we may proceed with an attempt to read Scripture humbly and carefully, "over against" ourselves, asking what acts and attitudes would be a little more fitting and faithful to the story.

White's essay attracted considerable attention — and considerable criticism.[3] Historians observed that the exploitation of nature is not unique to the West. Biblical scholars questioned White's interpretation of the relevant biblical passages. Theologians argued that the doctrine of creation was misjudged by White.

One of the earliest responses to White's essay was by Francis Schaeffer, a biblical inerrantist, who argued that, if Christians are to be faithful to the Bible and to the story of creation, they must not be arrogant masters of creation but its stewards. Indeed, the abuse of nature is the desecration of the creation and offensive to the Creator. Human beings, made in the im-

---

3. Among the major discussions of Lynn White's thesis are Ian Barbour, ed., *Western Man and Environmental Ethics: Attitudes towards Nature and Technology* (Reading, MA: Addison-Wesley, 1973), and David Spring and Eileen Spring, eds., *Ecology and Religion in History* (New York: Harper & Row, 1974).

age of God and responsible to God, are obliged to care for the creation.[4] One can evidently be a biblical inerrantist and accept as scientific fact an account of creation in six days and still question White's account of the story of creation and its implications. But one need not be. James Barr, for example, the eminent scholar of the Hebrew Bible, also argued against White's account of the creation story.[5] To be sure, there were some complex discussions about the meaning of *rada* ("have dominion") and *kabash* ("subdue").[6] And to be sure, there were some interesting conversations about the authority of Scripture relative to other sources of moral wisdom in the context of responses to White's thesis.[7] But Barr spoke for many

4. Francis Schaeffer, *Pollution and the Death of Man: The Christian View of Ecology* (Wheaton, IL: Tyndale House, 1973).

5. James Barr, "The Ecological Controversy and the Old Testament," *Bulletin of the John Rylands Library* 55 (1972): 9-32.

6. Contrast, for example, Lloyd H. Steffen, "In Defense of Dominion," *Environmental Ethics* 14 (1992): 63-80, for whom "dominion" . . . "is not a domination concept" with Wilhelm Fudpucker, "Through Christian Technology to Technological Christianity," in Carl Mitcham and Jim Grote, eds., *Theology and Technology: Essays in Christian Analysis and Exegesis* (New York: University Press of America, 1984), pp. 53-69, who insists that "subdue" be translated "to tread down," or "to conquer," or "to trample" (both cited by Peter Harrison, "Subduing the Earth: Genesis 1, Early Modern Science, and the Exploitation of Nature," *The Journal of Religion* [1999]: 86-109, p. 88). Some Christian environmentalists agree that the terms suggest domination even while they insist that domination is an inappropriate relation to nature. So, for example, Walter Wink, "Ecobible: The Bible and Ecojustice," *Theology Today* 49, no. 4 (1993): 472, who thinks "dominion" in Genesis 1:26 is "an unfortunate choice of words" that captured an ethos of domination over nature and that still sustains it. See further Louke van Wensveen Siker and the following note.

7. Louke van Wensveen Siker, "Environmentalists Read the Bible," in *Christian Ethics in Ecumenical Context*, ed. Shin Chiba, George R. Hunsberger, and Lester Edwin J. Ruiz (Grand Rapids: Eerdmans, 1995), pp. 207-

who disagreed with White's exegesis of Genesis when he acknowledged that "it is of course possible to argue that the Genesis account of creation has had an influence not through its
own original meaning but through interpretations which have
been placed upon it."[8] In the pursuit of that possibility the attention of historians shifted from the text itself to the frame-
works of interpretation that have been brought to the text —
and we turn our attention in that direction as well.

One important study of the history of interpretation of the
Genesis text, for example, made it clear that in the ancient
and medieval periods there was little to support White's
claim that Genesis 1:26-28 authorized the technological exploitation of nature.[9] Ancient and medieval interpreters read
the text allegorically, construing the vocation of "dominion
over the beasts" as a vocation to dominion over the beasts
within — over the passions. The allegorical interpretation of
the sacred text also informed the interpretation of nature.
Irenaeus, for example, had said that "earthly things should be
types of the celestial."[10] Natural objects were read as signs of

---

8, makes the interesting claim (supported by papers at a 1991 conference
on "Ecological Prospects: Theory and Practice" at Loyola Marymount University) that Protestant environmentalists disclosed a new interest in natural theology and Roman Catholic environmentalists found themselves
"searching the Scripture." Another piece of evidence that could be cited
for this methodological rapprochement is Charles M. Murphy, *At Home on
Earth: Foundations for a Catholic Ethic of the Environment* (New York: Cross-
road, 1989), which is a retrieval of the Genesis story.

8. Barr, "The Ecological Controversy," p. 23.

9. Jeremy Cohen, *"Be Fruitful and Increase, Fill the Earth and Master It":
The Ancient and Medieval Career of a Biblical Text* (Ithaca, NY: Cornell University Press, 1989). See also Peter Harrison, "Subduing the Earth," pp. 90-96.

10. Irenaeus, *Against Heresies* 4.19, in *Ante-Nicene Fathers* (Edinburgh:
T. & T. Clark, 1989), vol. 5, p. 439.

religious truths and moral lessons. To know nature in this context was to understand its moral and religious significance, not to exploit it.[11] It could well be claimed that the material world was valued instrumentally, as a means to spiritual truths, but it is evidently not the case that the text of Genesis 1 sponsored an attitude of exploitative dominion over nature in the ancient or medieval church.

The interpretative tradition was to shift in the seventeenth century, when the text did come to be read as a vocation to control nature. A variety of factors contributed to the shift in interpretation. Technological innovations themselves, with the performance of control over nature that they permitted and required, shaped a new attitude toward nature.[12] The truth seems to be that the shift in the interpretation of the Genesis text was prepared for by medieval technological developments, not that the Genesis texts themselves provided the ideological preparation for either arrogance toward nature or the development of technological mastery over nature.[13]

11. The Bestiaries, so popular in the Middle Ages, are examples of this approach to nature. They invest nature with profound (if frequently fanciful) meaning, testifying to a cosmic order in which human beings were the center of God's attention but in which human beings were hardly encouraged to the material exploitation of nature.

12. Consider, for example, White's claim that introduction of the heavy plow, which made large-scale agriculture possible, lifting it above subsistence farming, profoundly affected human attitudes to nature. According to White, this single development changed the relationship of human beings and nature: "Once man had been a part of nature; now he became her exploiter." Lynn White, Jr., *Medieval Technology and Social Change* (Oxford: Oxford University Press, 1966), p. 56.

13. White himself had earlier called attention to medieval attempts to master nature that were independent either of religious communities or of a religiously motivated ideology of the exploitation of nature (*Medieval Technology and Social Change*). There were, as White made clear, an im-

Another factor in the shift of interpretation was the fact that the sacramental symbolism that had informed the medieval Bestiaries gave way to an Aristotelian vitalism, which in turn gave way to a mechanistic view of the world. Perhaps the most important of these various factors, however, was a hermeneutic development in the sixteenth century that looked to the literal sense of the text as its true meaning (rather than to the symbolic or allegorical significance of the text).[14] That hermeneutic for the sacred text also informed the interpretation of nature; natural objects were no longer treated fundamentally as signs and symbols of spiritual and moral truths. The symbolic function of nature had to be replaced with some other function, and what better function than to serve human ends?

It was in the early modern period that the Genesis text came to be read and used as a justification and vocation for scientific and technological mastery over nature. Francis Bacon surely read and used the Genesis text in this way.[15] Ac-

---

pressive array of medieval machines that were introduced, but they were introduced without appeal to a religiously motivated ideology about "dominion" or the mastery of nature. They were evidently introduced to meet the needs for food and clothes and, when those needs were met, to satisfy the desire for some creature comforts.

14. See Peter Harrison, *The Bible, Protestantism, and the Rise of Natural Science* (Cambridge: Cambridge University Press, 1998). The literal reading of texts was given support by renaissance humanism and by the Protestant Reformation.

15. See Cameron Wybrow, *The Bible, Baconianism, and Mastery over Nature: The Old Testament and Its Modern Misreading* (New York: Peter Lang, 1991). It is the burden of Wybrow's book to show not only that Bacon read Genesis 1 in this way but also that it is a bad reading.

The Old Testament does indeed insist that nature is non-divine, but it does not, with the mastery writers, move hastily to the inference that nature is inanimate. In the Old Testament nature is responsive to both human and

cording to Bacon, the dominion over nature given with creation had been lost as a result of the fall, and human beings were being called to restore it in the seventeenth century. To quote him, "For man by the fall fell at the same time from his state of innocency and from his dominion over creation. Both of these losses however can even in this life be in some part repaired; the former by religion and faith, the latter by arts and sciences."[16] To repair the loss of dominion, to reestablish Adam's dominion, was made one of the objectives of the Royal Society.[17] Such mastery would require knowledge of nature (and of its causes and effects, not of its spiritual or moral significance), and Adam's naming of the animals was taken as a token of an encyclopedic knowledge that was also lost in the fall and now needed to be retrieved. Such mastery would also require work, and Adam's agricultural toil in dressing and keeping the garden was a token of that labor without which even the Garden of Eden could become a threatening desert or wilderness.

It seems, then, that with the rise of science at the beginning of the modern period there also arose a new reading of the Genesis story, a reading that made explicit connections between the mastery over (and exploitation of) nature and the story of creation. White's complaint about Scripture is misdirected. The problem is not with Scripture but with the interpretative arrogance of those at the beginning of the modern

divine action. . . . [M]ore important, it is utterly incompatible with the mechanistic view of nature of which it is alleged to be the root (pp. 197-98).

See also Peter Harrison, "Subduing the Earth."

16. Francis Bacon, *Novum Organum* 2.52, cited in Harrison, "Subduing the Earth," p. 98.

17. Thomas Sprat, *History of the Royal Society* (London, 1667), p. 62; see Harrison, "Subduing the Earth," p. 98.

period who read Scripture in self-serving defense of their project of the mastery of nature. White's complaint about the Western exploitation of nature makes some sense against the background of the seventeenth century, but his contrast between a "pagan" attitude toward nature and a "biblical" attitude toward nature is less significant than the contrast between an ancient attitude and a modern attitude.

Moreover, as Peter Harrison has argued, things were even more complex in the seventeenth century.[18] For one thing, the anthropocentrism often associated with exploitative attitudes toward nature was no less characteristic of the ancient and medieval periods than of the modern period. Indeed, the seventeenth century witnessed the first serious challenges to anthropocentrism in the West. It was science itself that taught us that we are not "the center of the universe." However, science could not teach us where we do belong. As Nietzsche would aptly put it, "since Copernicus man has been rolling from the center into x."[19] Human beings and their earth were once at the center. They did not put themselves there; God put them there, and it was simply accepted as a matter of course that they were there. After Copernicus had shown that they were not at the center, humanity was left to fend for itself (or simply to continue "rolling"). This positionlessness became the new assumption, and it entailed that humanity had to attempt to secure (if somewhat anxiously) a place for itself — and what better place than at the center? After Copernicus, humanity was not simply at the center, it had to put itself at the center, make itself into the center. If anthropocentrism

18. See Harrison, "Subduing the Earth," pp. 102-9.

19. Cited in Eberhard Jüngel, *God as the Mystery of the World,* trans. Darrell Guder (Grand Rapids: Eerdmans, 1983), p. 15.

was to survive, it would have to change its character from being received as a given to being assertively achieved.

Moreover, the scientific criticism of explanations of nature that invoked "final causes" left nature no longer oriented to human wellbeing. Human needs and desires were not served by the nature of nature, oriented to final causes that included human wellbeing. So, it was less anthropocentrism than the new doubts about the cosmic status of human beings that motivated the effort to master an uncooperative nature. The very science that destroyed the illusions that humanity was at the center and that nature was ordered toward human wellbeing fortunately gave to humanity power in the world and over the world. Such mastery, however, would not succeed in eliminating human insecurity and anxiety; in fact, the new powers and their unintended consequences would consistently evoke new anxieties.

There is another complication. Bacon and the "Royal Society" may have misread the Genesis texts in the interest of their project, but they were not altogether out of touch with the story of Scripture. This explains a feature of the seventeenth-century reading of the Genesis story that subsequent centuries (and what we have called the Baconian project) too often overlooked. For Bacon the dominion sought was a dominion lost in the fall. Moreover, according to Bacon the fall and the curse that came in its wake left its mark not only on humanity but also on nature. As a result of human sin "the ground" was cursed (Gen. 3:17); the natural world, too, was fallen. The attitude toward nature was complicated by a distinction between the "natural" world as created and the "natural" world as disfigured and fallen. Bacon regarded the recovery of Adam's dominion not as a human tyranny over nature but as the restoration of nature to its pre-fallen order and goodness. As John

Donne put it, "our business is, to rectify nature, to what she was."[20] The attitude toward nature here was not an arrogant indifference to nature's good but a careful concern to restore nature to its own perfection.[21] Indeed, Peter Harrison suggests that Bacon might be retrieved against the consequences of what we have called the Baconian project.

> However ecologically naïve our seventeenth-century forebears might now appear, and however misguided their efforts to "improve" the natural world, their program of retrieving a nature that had fallen into ruin on account of human transgressions seems not entirely inappropriate for the late twentieth [or early twenty-first] century.[22]

The problem is not Scripture but the interpretative arrogance of those who would interpret Scripture. The result of interpretative arrogance is, as we said above, frequently the abuse of Scripture, and then the abuse of others, usually the weak and powerless, by means of the abuse of Scripture. In this context interpretative arrogance has led to the abuse of Scripture and the abuse of nature by means of the abuse of Scripture. The best corrective to interpretative arrogance is frequently to read Scripture in Christian community, to listen to Scripture while listening to the voices of the marginalized and power-

---

20. John Donne, "To Sir Edward Herbert at Julyers," in *Donne* (New York: Dell, 1962), p. 103.

21. Harrison argues that during the seventeenth century at least the distinction between attitudes of "dominion" and "stewardship" is nonexistent.

22. Harrison, "Subduing the Earth," p. 109.

less. And in this context the best corrective is to read Scripture while listening to the "groaning" of the creation (Rom. 8:22).

There is, of course, always a framework of interpretation that is brought to the text of Scripture, as the historians have reminded us. As there is no "view from nowhere,"[23] so there is no interpretation that escapes the influence of the reader's historical and social location. And the following effort is no exception. There is a risk of simply using Scripture to defend a contemporary ecological agenda. Two things make the risk of a fresh reading of Scripture worth taking. The first is the recognition that the framework of interpretation may never be substituted for the text itself in Christian communities, joined to the confidence that the text of Scripture, and the story it tells, can challenge even the framework of interpretation that is brought to it.[24] The second is this: the authority of Scripture for the Christian life. Christian ethics still proceeds by way of reminder. The Christian community must constantly revisit and retrieve the sacred story to assess and to challenge both existing interpretations and alternative stories or mythoi. If every *ethos* has its *mythos,* then the task of retrieving the biblical story is normatively significant for the

23. Thomas Nagel, *The View from Nowhere* (New York: Oxford University Press, 1986).

24. As the Old Testament scholar Bernard Anderson said,

Clearly, we read the Bible "where we are": as people who are conditioned by the times in which we live and by the history that we share. . . . This sober realization does not, in my estimation, mire us in interpretive relativism. . . . To be sure, we come to the Scriptures in a particular time and place. But the words of Scripture . . . may criticize where we stand, limit our use of them, and challenge us with their strange social setting and theological horizon" (Bernard Anderson, *From Creation to New Creation* [Minneapolis: Augsburg Fortress, 1994], p. 134).

consideration both of nature and of the goals and limits for altering it. But let us read it humbly, ready to be challenged by it rather than to use it to defend ourselves and the projects dear to us, attentive to the voices of all those who suffer, including the creation.

IV

An Alternative Mythos *and* Ethos: *Revisiting the Christian Story*

Christian ethics proceeds "by way of reminder." That is just to follow the example of Paul, who wrote to the Roman churches "by way of reminder" (Rom. 15:15). He reminded them of "the gospel of God" (1:1) in order to bring about "the obedience of faith" (1:5; 16:26). The first rule for Christian ethics ought always to be "Remember!"

"Remember!" Little wonder, then, that Christian ethics is intimately related to the reading of Scripture. It is by reading Scripture that the church remembers the story that gives it an identity and makes it a community. It is by reading Scripture together that the church remembers the story that they would use in their communities to test whether their character and their conduct are "worthy of the gospel," whether they fit the story they love to tell and long to live. Reading Scripture together is not the only way the churches remember, but it is surely a critically important way for any Christian ethic that would proceed "by way of reminder." Christians read Scripture in order to remember, and that memory is constitutive for identity and determinative for discernment.

There is more to Scripture than story, of course. There are legal statutes and wisdom precepts. There are prophetic oracles and apocalyptic visions. There are letters and pastoral advice. But all of it in the Christian canon is set in the context of a grand narrative that moves from the creation of all things to the renewal of "all things" (Rev. 21:5) and that finds its center in the story of Jesus of Nazareth. The story has hermeneutical and moral priority. The rules, precepts, and advice that are found in Scripture are normative in the Christian community not as timeless moral truths but as parts of the story. The story, of course, holds us to many of them, but it also requires us to continue to test them by whether they still fit the story. Within Scripture itself, the statutes were sometimes changed; what was received as conventional wisdom was sometimes challenged, and pastoral advice was sometimes offered to a community for its own storied discernment. The continuing church may and must continue to test its received moral tradition, including the rules it finds in Scripture, by whether they are still worthy of the gospel, whether they still fit the story. To give just one obvious example, the rules concerning slavery were modified within Scripture to make them a little more fitting to a story of the Exodus and of a God who heard the cries of the poor. And in the church, if tardily, the story finally required rules that did not simply regulate slavery but prohibited it.[1]

1. See further Allen Verhey, *Remembering Jesus: Christian Community, Scripture, and the Moral Life* (Grand Rapids: Eerdmans, 2002), pp. 3-13 and 49-76, where this account of Christian ethics "by way of reminder" and this proposal for the relation of Scripture to Christian ethics are described and defended. *Remembering Jesus* continued with an effort to bring the

And there is more to Christian ethics than narrative, of course. Jim Gustafson has helpfully distinguished four "varieties of moral discourse" in Christian ethics, not only "narrative discourse" but also "prophetic discourse" and "ethical discourse" and "policy discourse."[2] There are still the voices of prophets and the wisdom of sages; there are still the conversations concerning the analysis of our moral terms and the "art of the possible" in our politics. But all of it, I hold, is funded by the narrative and finally tested by the story. I will return to some of these other forms of discourse in the final chapter, but first I would revisit the Christian story, the *mythos,* that locates us and orients us, that forms character and community, and that may reform our attitudes toward nature and altering it.

1. Beginning "in the Beginning": The Creation Story

To begin at the beginning — "in the beginning" God created all things. The Christian Scripture starts where the Jewish Scripture starts — with the creation narrative.

It might have been otherwise. Marcion came to Rome around 140, proclaiming the gospel as he understood it. Mar-

---

church's memory and Scripture's story to bear upon our world of sickness and suffering, our world of sex and gender, our economic world, and our political world. More than one friend and critic observed that an obvious lacuna in that book was an effort to bring the church's memory and the Scripture's story to bear on ecology. This little book is an effort to supply that missing piece.

2. James M. Gustafson, "Varieties of Moral Discourse: Prophetic, Narrative, Ethical, and Policy," in *Seeking Understanding: The Stob Lectures, 1986-1998* (Grand Rapids: Eerdmans, 2001), pp. 46-76.

cion claimed that Jesus, far from being an agent of the God who had created the world and covenanted with Israel at Sinai, had delivered humanity from that creator, lawgiver, and judge — and from the hold that that God had on humanity through the body. Correlative with such a theology was Marcion's rejection of the Hebrew Scriptures as canon for the church. In its place he proposed an abridged Gospel of Luke and the Pauline epistles. And correlative to both such a canon and such a theology was Marcion's indifference and enmity to both this world and to the body. Marcion (mis)understood Paul's contrast between the "flesh" and the "spirit" to entail animosity to the body and to the creation, and he insisted on a rigorous asceticism from his followers.

The church said "no" to Marcion, "no" to his canon, "no" to his theology, and "no" to his view of creation and the body. This response hastened the development of both canon and creed. The canon would (continue to) include the Hebrew Scriptures as Christian Scripture, and it would include a larger collection of "New Testament" writings. The Apostles' Creed would summarize the story of Scripture and govern the reading of it, beginning with the affirmation that the Creator was the Redeemer, that the God who made this world was the very God who sent Jesus to liberate it.

"I believe in God the Father Almighty, maker of heaven and earth." Against Marcion Christians owned this story as their story in both canon and creed and committed themselves to lives somehow fitting to it. God is the Creator, "the maker of heaven and earth," that is to say, of everything, that is to say, of nature.

To begin "in the beginning," however, we need not — and should not — forget the rest of the story. When we do, then we tend to make the story simply a story of origins, as if it were prompted by a scientific curiosity about the order and circumstances that accompanied the origin of the world. It is a *mythos,* and it forms an *ethos.* It is not just that God *was* the creator but that God *is* the Creator. It is not just that once upon a time long ago God displayed his power and grace but that God displays his power and grace even now as Creator and seeks a fitting response. The rest of the story may remind us that the Creator God is the God of Israel, the God who makes covenant and keeps covenant, the God who enters into relationships with what God has made, whether a people or a world, delights in them, sometimes suffers for the sake of them, unfailingly keeps his promises with respect to them. The rest of the story may remind us that the Creator God is the triune God, that the same self-giving love of God's own life is at work in the creation, that the powerful and creative Word (John 1:1-4) was and is active in creation, that the life-giving Spirit of God is the very Spirit once and still active in creation. The triune God is still at work. The end of the story of creation is God's good future. The whole story shapes our identity and our discernment, our response to God and to the creation of God.

Still, the whole story cannot be told at once. So, to begin "in the beginning" . . .

a. Nature Is Not God . . .
but Not an Abandoned Artifact Either

Because God is the creator of all things, Christians have always echoed the Jewish prohibition of idols. If God made all things, then nothing God made is God. One may own the story of creation and think it took longer than seven days, but one may not own this story and think the creation, or any part of it, to be God. The story does not permit idolatry. There is a narrative prohibition of idolatry in the story of creation, a radical monotheism.

Nothing God made is God — neither the light nor "the lights," neither the natural powers of fertility and procreation nor the human capacities for freedom and the "dominion" of nature, neither nature nor the power to alter it, nothing. When we are tempted by the Baconian project to extravagant and idolatrous expectations of technology, this *mythos* calls us back from idolatry. And when, in reaction to the Baconian project, we are tempted to make natural processes — or the whole biotic "system" — sacrosanct, as though "Mother Nature" were God, this *mythos* calls us back from idolatry.[3] The story calls Jews and Christians to turn from idols.

The point can be — and should be — put positively. It is God who is God, God alone who is God. The story not only prohibits idolatry; it invites a radical confidence in God and a radical loyalty to the cause of God. The story calls human beings to relate to God alone as God and then "to relate to all things in a manner appropriate to their relations to God."[4]

3. Certain accounts of "deep ecology" are susceptible to this charge of idolatry. People like J. Baird Callicott do well to remind us that nature as a whole is good, but when they make nature (or the good of the whole biotic community) the "center of value," to use H. Richard Niebuhr's term, then they are perilously close to idolatry. Then human beings and individual animals only have value insofar as they contribute to the wellbeing of the whole biotic community. See the quote from Callicott in chapter II, pp. 43-44.

4. James M. Gustafson, *Ethics from a Theocentric Perspective,* vol. 1: *Theology and Ethics* (Chicago: University of Chicago Press, 1981), pp. 113 et passim. See also Gustafson, *A Sense of the Divine: The Natural Environment from a Theocentric Perspective* (Cleveland: Pilgrim Press, 1994), p. 148.

The story is *theocentric,* and so should story-formed thoughts about nature — and about "altering" it — be.

A theocentric perspective will reject the assumption that the world is finally autonomous and independent, and it will reject the assumption that the world, or nature, is divine. It rejects both the naturalism that empties the world of mystery and grace and the romanticism that invests the creation with divine status. It stands as an alternative both to an anthropocentrism that reduces nature to its utility to humanity and to a biocentrism that elevates nature to the status of God and rejects the distinctiveness of the human creature.

This theocentric story invites humanity, first, to acknowledge its own distinctive responsiveness (and responsibility) to God as a member of a larger whole, as part of the whole creation, and second, to acknowledge their non-human neighbors as creatures of the same God.[5]

The creation story in Genesis 1 (1:1–2:4a) was first written, I think, during the Babylonian exile and as a polemical re-

<hr />

5. See, for example, Jürgen Moltmann, *God in Creation: A New Theology of Creation and the Spirit of God,* trans. Margaret Kohl (San Francisco: Harper & Row, 1985), p. 31. Moltmann, no less than Gustafson, reads the biblical materials as displaying and requiring a theocentric perspective. Many others have called attention to the *theocentrism* of the biblical perspective and have contrasted it to both anthropocentrism and biocentrism. See, e.g., Steven Bouma-Prediger, *The Greening of Theology: The Ecological Models of Rosemary Radford Ruether, Joseph Sittler, and Jürgen Moltmann* (Oxford: Oxford University Press, 2000), pp. 278-79, and works cited there, including Paul Santmire, *Brother Earth: Nature, Man, and God in Time of Crisis* (New York: Thomas Nelson, 1970), chapters 1 and 2; Wesley Granberg-Michaelson, "Renewing the Whole Creation," *Sojourners* (February-March 1990); Richard Young, *Healing the Earth: A Theocentric Perspective on Environmental Problems and Their Solutions* (Nashville: Broadman & Holman, 1994).

sponse to the Babylonian epic of creation, the *Enuma Elish.* In striking contrast to the Babylonian epic, this story has one God rather than many gods, and moreover, that one God is not identified with primeval nature or any part of it. In the Babylonian epic Marduk, the king of the gods, was primeval light. In Genesis 1 God made the light — and "the lights" (but not, as in *Enuma Elish,* as homes to the astral deities).

The creation story famously — or infamously, according to Lynn White, Jr. — "desacralized" nature, "disenchanted" it. "Disenchanted," however, may be too strong, for neither this story nor the larger narrative renders nature simply an "it." The creation story will not permit idolatry, but it does not empty the world of "animism"; it does not render nature a machine. It does not deny a continuing and intimate relationship between God and nature. God is continuously present to the creation, involved in its life, and the creation continuously manifests God's power and grace. Nature is not simply God's abandoned artifact. In the first place, the creation is not abandoned. God upholds it and sustains it. The story of creation is a continuing story, not just a story about "origins." The "laws of nature" are simply the way God ordinarily works to uphold and sustain the creation. In the second place, the creation is not simply artifact. It is dynamic and responsive. The creation is not God, but it manifests God and "declares the glory of God."[6] There is a mysterious activity as the non-human parts of creation respond to God's call to be. To quote my friend and colleague from Hope College, Steve Bouma-Prediger, "All creatures respond to the call of God to be and to

6. That is why John Calvin, who was hardly sympathetic with idolatry, could acknowledge that "it can be said reverently, provided it proceeds from a reverent mind, that nature is God." *Institutes,* I.v.5. (In I.v.4 Calvin had rejected the idolatry of nature.)

become, each in their own creature-specific way."[7] When the psalmist invites all creatures in heaven and on earth to praise God (Psalm 148)[8] and when the same psalm describes the winds as "fulfilling [God's] command" (v. 8), it is possible to "demythologize" such passages, but before we do, we should observe that the biblical *mythos* does not construe nature as an unresponsive artifact but a responsive and dynamic community of creatures.[9]

b. Nature Is Good . . . but Not Perfect

Nothing God made is god, but all that God made is good. This is the second implication of the creation story. One may own this story and think creation took a path that included evolutionary processes, fulfilling God's command (like the winds, Ps. 148:8), but one may not own this story and think the world God made is not good. All that God made is good. God says as much in the story, of course. "God saw everything that he had made, and indeed, it was very good" (Gen. 1:31). The light and "the lights" are good. The natural powers of fertility and procreation are good. The human capacities for freedom and "dominion" are good gifts of God. And life, in its finitude and

---

7. Bouma-Prediger, *The Greening of Theology,* p. 281. He cites several theologians who make this point about the "responsiveness" of the creation. See also Richard Fern, *Nature, God and Humanity: Envisioning an Ethics of Nature* (Cambridge: Cambridge University Press, 2002), p. 204.

8. The choir of creaturely voices in Psalm 148 is quite magnificently expanded in the *Benedicte,* the apocryphal addition to Daniel at Daniel 3:23, "The Song of the Three Young Men."

9. See Appendix A for an account of various typologies for the relation of God and nature.

dependence upon God, is good. All that God made is good. When the Baconian project tempts us to regard nature itself as the enemy, and our finitude itself as our flaw, then this *mythos* orients us to affirm the good creation of God.

There is, moreover, nothing in the story to suggest that "good" *means* simply "useful for human beings." The refrain that what God made is "good" is repeated several times before the creation of human beings. And the refrain echoes through the rest of Scripture as well. When Psalm 104 celebrates the creation, for example, it delights, to be sure, in the "plants for people to use," the "wine to gladden the human heart," and the "bread to strengthen" it (Ps. 104:14-15). But it delights as well in the things and events where people are absent but where God's care is surely present.

> The trees of the Lord are watered abundantly, the cedars of Lebanon that he planted. In them the birds build their nests; the stork has its home in the fir trees. The high mountains are for the wild goats; the rocks are a refuge for the coneys. (Ps. 104:16-18)

There is no suggestion that the cedars and the birds or the goats and the badgers are there for the sake of human beings. God cares for them and delights in them; they are good.[10]

The contrast with the Babylonian creation epic may once more be instructive. In the *Enuma Elish* the identification of primeval nature with the gods does not authorize the judgment that nature is good, for the gods themselves are good and evil. Marduk, who is identified with primeval light (and with the rulers of Babylon), is good. Tiamat, who is identified

---

10. See also Job 38-39.

with the waters of chaos that threaten humanity, is evil. Moreover, in the *Enuma Elish* creation takes place with an act of violence. Marduk, primeval light, slays Tiamat, the waters of chaos, with a lightning bolt into her belly. Then he splits her in two, dividing the waters, and sets up the firmament as a barrier. Although there are echoes of the battle against the watery forces of chaos in the biblical materials (e.g., Ps. 74:12-17; 89:10; Isa. 27:1; 51:9), the story of Genesis 1 is striking for its account of a peaceable beginning and of peaceable difference within the creation. In Genesis 1 the light, created the first day, is not God, but it is good. And when the waters are separated from the waters on the second day, it is not an act of violence but a response to God's command. God speaks the firmament and the separation of the waters into existence, summons it into existence with a word. Nature is not god, but precisely in its creaturely otherness from God and in its dependence upon God it is good, all of it.

Consider Job 40:1–41:34, God's response to Job's accusations "out of the whirlwind." There God describes the creatures Behemoth and Leviathan, creatures who live in the water like hippopotami and crocodiles but also live in legend, creatures associated with the chaotic. The reader expects God to vanquish them, to destroy them, to split them in two, to destroy them, like Marduk did Tiamat. They are evil and threatening. But God does not destroy them; he simply describes them, and rather playfully at that. And why? Job has accused God, impugned the way God runs the world, prepared to condemn God in order to defend his own righteousness. God's reply begins by inviting Job to imagine that Job is God, that he is clothed "with glory and splendor" (40:10), and that he could act the way he thinks God should act, "to play God," if you will, to dominate and to destroy these creatures, to vanquish them, to abase the proud and avenge the wrong (40:11-13). Perhaps the world would be better if Job ran things. But then God begins to describe Behemoth and Leviathan.

The description serves to confront Job with his own pride and with the folly of his fantasy of domination. They are fearsome creatures, to be sure, and Job would be no match for them. But they are not described as evil. Behemoth is described as "the first of the great acts of God." It is a powerful creature; "only its Maker can approach it with the sword" (Job 40:19). But no sword is drawn; no battle is fought. The powerful Behemoth is described as resting peacefully in the marsh (v. 21). Leviathan is an even more dangerous and even more magnificent creature. "Who can confront it and be safe? — under the whole heaven, who?" (Job 41:11). Again God does not destroy the creature as evil. The terrible Leviathan is described with something like the pride of a craftsman telling of his work and with something like delight as it sports in the water.[11] "It surveys everything that is lofty; it is king over all that are proud" (Job 41:34). That is enough for Job to retract his accusation and to repent of the pride that presumed to know better than God. Now he is indeed one who serves God because God is God and not because it pays. Now he is indeed one who serves God "for nothing" (Job 1:9), not unlike the clouds and the waves.

Although God does not proceed with violence and domination, Job knows "no purpose of [God's] can be thwarted" (Job 42:2). It is the fruit of that repentance when Job prays for his friends, reconciled with his accusers. It is the fruit of that repentance when, in spite of the hard reminders of the fragility of life, he trusted God and the goodness of God's creation

11. Also in Psalm 104:26 Leviathan is described as "sporting" in the sea, something like the Loch Ness monster.

enough to have more children. It is the fruit of that repentance when, against the conventional assumptions of patriarchy and its distribution of power and privilege, he gave his daughters as well as his sons an inheritance (Job 42:7-17). And it is not too much to suppose that also among the fruits of his repentance was a less arrogant attitude toward nature, a humble readiness to acknowledge its goodness.[12]

Nature is good, then, in God's reply to Job. But in Job's world and in ours there is the possibility of "natural evil."[13] Where crocodiles live and where winds blow, there is the possibility of "natural evil." Great winds can destroy life, for example (Job 1:19). And a crocodile is a predator, after all. And we can hardly avoid the question whether "natural evil" was given with the creation itself, even if Behemoth and Leviathan are not called evil creatures. A variety of answers have been given to this problem of "natural evil" before the fall of Adam.

One traditional answer asserted that there was no "natural evil," no death, no suffering, no predation, until human sin brought the curse not only upon humanity but upon the whole creation.[14] That answer, however, now seems quite implausible. Some animals were evidently carnivores long before human beings arrived on the scene. Recognizing this, C. S. Lewis proposed an answer that seems to me to be at least as implau-

---

12. On Job see further especially Carol A. Newsom, "The Moral Sense of 'Nature': Ethics in the Light of God's Speech in Job," *The Princeton Seminary Bulletin* 15, no. 1 (1994): 9-27. See also Bill McKibben, *The Comforting Whirlwind: God, Job, and the Scale of Creation* (Cambridge: Cowley, 2005); and Steven Bouma-Prediger, *For the Beauty of the Earth: A Christian Vision for Creation Care* (Grand Rapids: Baker Academic, 2001), pp. 100-105.

13. My thanks to Uko Zylstra of Calvin College for raising this question of "natural evil" and predation when the Jellema lectures were delivered.

14. It is important to say, of course, that predation and death are not a "moral evil." That only enters the creation with human sin.

sible. He proposed a series of rebellions against God, beginning with the rebellion of a mighty angel. That mighty and rebellious angel was already "at work for ill" in the world before the creation of human beings, and it "corrupted the animal creation before man appeared."[15] A third answer, and the one I prefer, is that "natural evil" and death and predation are simply part of the good creation.[16] This answer is hardly a new response. Psalm 104, the hymn to God the Creator to which we have already referred, evidently "understands the 'preying' of the lion as a kind of 'praying'":[17] "The young lions roar for their prey, seeking their food from God" (v. 21). And in the fourth century Basil the Great commended nature, including predation, as "a wise and marvelous order," even observing that God had given to carnivorous animals the "pointed teeth which their nature requires for their support."[18] And the great Thomas Aquinas in the thirteenth century took the position that "man's sin did not so change the nature of animals, that those whose nature it is now to eat other animals, like lions and hawks, would then have lived on a vegetable diet."[19]

15. C. S. Lewis, *The Problem of Pain* (New York: Macmillan, 1962), pp. 133-36. I do not find Lewis's suggestion implausible so much because of the hypothesis of a rebellious angel (although I do not see any evidence of it in the story) but because I do not see why God would not have protected his good creation from the corruption of these rebellious angels.

16. See Fern, *Nature, God and Humanity,* pp. 216-23.

17. Patrick D. Miller, Jr., "The Poetry of Creation: Psalm 104," in William P. Brown and S. Dean McBride, Jr., eds., *God Who Creates: Essays in Honor of W. Sibley Towner* (Grand Rapids: Eerdmans, 2000), p. 98.

18. Basil the Great, "Hexameron," in *Letters and Selected Writings,* vol. 8 of *Select Library of the Christian Church: Nicene and Post-Nicene Fathers,* trans. Blomfield Jackson (Peabody, MA: Hendrickson, 1995), pp. 92, 105.

19. Thomas Aquinas, *Summa Theologica,* I, Q. 96, a. 1 (Blackfriars edition, New York: McGraw-Hill, 1964), vol. 8, p. 125.

But if there is death and predation in the creation, may we still echo God's declaration that "it is good"? Look at the lion. Surely God's declaration fits the lion. It is good, even if it is hard to think of a lion without thinking predator. Or consider the antelope. Surely God's declaration fits the antelope. It is good, even if it is hard to think antelope (especially in such close proximity to the lion) without thinking prey. But consider again the lion, now "red in tooth and claw" with the blood of the antelope. Can we say this is good? Not by itself. By itself it counts as "natural evil." But in the context of what makes the lion a lion and an antelope an antelope we may echo God's declaration. The mighty lion has its terrible beauty, like Behemoth and Leviathan, but the antelope has its grace, speed, and alertness, and these are developed and displayed in its struggle to survive. They would not be the magnificent creatures they are apart from a nature that includes predation. It does make sense to call the life of the lion good and the life of the antelope good and to echo — over a nature that includes predation — God's declaration that "it is good."

That is not to say, however, that the pain and death of the antelope are by themselves good or that the pain and death of any animal is good. The deep ecologist J. Baird Callicott draws that conclusion: "That is the way the system works. If nature as a whole is good, then pain and death are also good."[20] It counts rather, I think, as "natural evil." To be sure, pain alerts an animal to bodily injury, and death seems given with the creation, the flip side of the blessing upon the creatures, "Be fruitful and multiply" (Gen. 1:22). And to be sure, the non-human creature does not reflect about its death, does not

20. J. Baird Callicott, "Animal Liberation: A Triangular Affair," *Environmental Ethics* 2 (Winter 1980): 333.

contemplate it as the end to projects and plans with which it identifies. We can admit that death has a less frightening significance for non-human creatures than it does for human creatures (at least after the fall).[21] All of this, however, does not make the death and suffering of an animal a good, even if it may make it relatively less "evil." The "system" is good, but the death and suffering of an animal is tragic. It is regrettable even if necessary in this good creation.

We seem driven to admit that the creation is good . . . but not yet perfect. We can hardly imagine what the perfection of a good creation would be. The prophet Isaiah suggested that it will mean an end to predation, the lion lying down with lambs and antelopes (Isa. 11:6-9; 65:25). The prophet Hosea imagined "a covenant on that day with all the wild animals, the birds of the air, and the creeping things upon the ground" (Hos. 2:18). Ezekiel's vision (Ezek. 34:25-27) is not that the wolf and the lamb will feed together but that the predatory animals will be banished from the land (see also Lev. 26:6).[22] There is obviously a problem of diversity in these eschatological visions. Nevertheless, they agree in this, that the perfection of the creation will be the work of God, the fulfilling of the work God began in the creation, the completion of the work that God continues by sustaining a good creation in

21. We will return to the death of human creatures below, pp. 87-88.

22. These visions should not be read as literal descriptions of the future (or of the beginnings). Moreover, these visions of God's good future are surely conditioned by the simple fact that wild animals are a problem for people engaged in farming and herding. Nevertheless, their common confidence is in a God who promises a "covenant of peace" (Ezek. 34:25) and a blessing that is cosmic in scope. On these passages see further W. Sibley Towner, "The Future of Nature," *Interpretation* 50 (1996): 27-35, and Gene M. Tucker, "The Peaceable Kingdom and a Covenant with Wild Animals," in Brown and McBride, eds., *God Who Creates*, pp. 215-25.

spite of human sin. The good future of God that surpasses our imagination will be the work of a God who fulfills the promise of creation, a "covenant of peace" (Ezek. 34:25) that brings the blessing of peace to the nations and to the whole biotic community. It will be the good future of God. In the meanwhile nature is good . . . but not yet perfect. God goes on working, and God can be trusted; "no purpose of [God's] can be thwarted" (Job 42:2).

c. Humanity Part of Nature . . . and Distinguished Within It

There is a great divide in the story of creation, but it is not between human beings and "nature," or the rest of the creation, nor is it between the human body (as part of "nature") and some divine spark or immortal soul in humanity. The great divide is between God and God's creation, and human beings stand wholly on this side of that divide, part of nature, not simply transcendent over it. Still, there is a distinction in the story between the rest of the creation and humanity. The distinction is marked by the creation of male and female in *"the image of God"* (Gen. 1:26-27).

This notion of "the image of God" has been fundamental to Christian theological anthropology.[23] It has been, of course, interpreted in various ways. Let it be admitted that there is a

23. Hendrikus Berkhof, for example, suggests that a substantial piece of the history of ideas in the West could be written by attending to what theologians have said about this notion. See Berkhof, *Christian Faith,* trans. S. Woudstra (Grand Rapids: Eerdmans, 1979), p. 179. See also Emil Brunner, *Man in Revolt,* trans. O. Wyon (New York: Charles Scribner's Sons, 1939), p. 92. For a catalog of interpretations, see Brunner, pp. 498-515.

long tradition that not only made "the image of God" central to theological anthropology but also identified it with human capacities for self-awareness and self-determination, with the "faculties" of intelligence and will. And let it also be admitted that beginning in the seventeenth century the "image of God" was sometimes simply identified with "dominion."[24] But let it also be admitted that such traditions of interpretation must also be tested by the Scripture they attempt to understand.[25]

In the beginning by God's word human beings were created as "the image of God" (Gen. 1:26-27). Once again it may be helpful to read the story in contrast to the *Enuma Elish*. Genesis 1 was, as we have said, probably written in exile in self-conscious polemic against the Babylonian creation epic. We have already drawn attention to the different views of God

24. See D. Hall, *Imaging God: Dominion as Stewardship* (Grand Rapids: Eerdmans, 1986), pp. 89-98.

25. There are few references to "the image of God" in Scripture, and they are mostly cryptic. The notion appears, of course, in the creation story (in the priestly account of that story, Gen. 1:26-27), and in the Hebrew Scriptures only twice more (Gen. 5:1-3 and 9:5-6). The notion appears more frequently in the New Testament, where — significantly — it usually refers to Christ or to the church (Rom. 8:29; 1 Cor. 11:7, 15:49; 2 Cor. 3:18, 4:4; Col. 1:15, 3:10; Heb. 1:3; James 3:9). None of these references identify the "image" with human powers of reason and choice and dominion or contrast the "image" to human bodies. If one gleans from these passages hints of the ways human beings can "image" God or are "something like" God, one finds not one but a host of human excellencies: dominion (Gen. 1:26), relationships of mutuality and equality (Gen. 1:27), fruitfulness (Gen. 5:1-3), conformity to Christ (Rom. 8:29), and all the virtues, "the concretely visible sanctification" that such conformity requires (G. C. Berkouwer, *Man: The Image of God* [Grand Rapids: Eerdmans, 1962], p. 112). The ways of human imaging of God are many and varied in Scripture, but none of them are disembodied. And in none of them are we solitary individuals. The whole person in community is created and renewed in "the image of God."

and nature in these stories, but consider also the views of humanity. In the *Enuma Elish* Marduk made "man" from the blood of Kingu, a defeated and evil god. He made "man," moreover, for service to the gods (and their representatives in Babylon). But Genesis 1 told a different story, a story in which God alone is God, a story in which nature is not divine, *and* a story in which God makes "man" (male and female) not from the blood of an evil god but as God's own "image," and not for bondage but for freedom, not to be slave but to rule.

One may own this story and think the order may have been a little different, but one may not own this story and think a man fit for slavery or reduce a woman to her utility. That human beings are created in the image of God is the narrative basis for the prohibition against murder in Genesis 9:6.[26] From the beginning this *mythos* orients us to respect the special dignity of the human being. It resists the reduction of any, including those with whom we are procreating or those whom we are procreating, to their utility, to their service to our projects, whether the project is parenting or scientific mastery.[27]

But the story not only calls for a special respect for the human creature in addition to a regard for nature, it also suggests the vocation of the human creature in the midst of the creation. That image of an "image," a *tselem,* a statue, was borrowed from the practice of earthly monarchs who set up

26. Genesis 9:6, like the first creation story, is attributed to the priestly source of the Torah, or P.

27. This orientation is relevant, of course, to a faithful consideration of altering natural processes of begetting and to embryonic stem cell research and to much besides, but we leave such consideration aside. See Allen Verhey, *Reading the Bible in the Strange World of Medicine* (Grand Rapids: Eerdmans, 2003), pp. 253-303.

images of themselves in their realm as a sign of their own sovereign authority. It is in this sense that the human being was made as "the image of God."[28] God set human beings in the midst of the creation to be a sign of God's own care and rule. They signal God's rule by their very physical presence and, yes, by ruling — but only by ruling in ways that honor God's cause and reflect God's way. To be God's "image" is to receive a vocation to make manifest God's rule.[29]

d. A Vocation to Image God's Care

To be God's "image," we said, is to receive a vocation to make God's rule manifest. And how shall humanity image God the Creator in relation to nature? How can humanity make manifest God's rule in the creation? How can human beings reflect God's ways also in "altering nature"?

There are some clues, I think, about what it would mean to image God in relation to the rest of nature within the creation story itself. If I read the story right, to image God the Creator might mean something too much overlooked in a science formed by the Baconian project. It might mean that we look at the creation, at nature, and say to ourselves, "God, that's good." It might mean, that is, first of all, to *wonder,* to stand in awe, to delight in the elegant structure of the creation, its dynamic interdependence, its fragile balance. It would mean a celebration of knowledge that is not simply mastery. It would

28. Following Gerhard von Rad, *Old Testament Theology,* vol. 1: *The Theology of Israel's Historical Traditions,* trans. D. Stalker (New York: Harper & Row, 1962), pp. 144-47.

29. See Appendix B for an account of typologies for the relation of nature and humanity.

mean an appreciation of nature — including human nature — as given, rather than a suspicion of nature as threatening and requiring human mastery. It would mean a reorientation toward nature, a turning from the myth of the Baconian project with respect to it. Indeed, without such admiration for the work of God, without such awe before the Creator, human beings are tempted to reduce human progress to technological progress and to alienate themselves from the creation on which they depend and for which they have the vocation to care. This *mythos* orients us not only toward "stewardship"[30] but also and fundamentally to wonder and celebration. The first response, and the first responsibility, to God the Creator is gratitude, and gratitude includes delight.

And if I read the story right, to image God might mean a second thing too much overlooked. It might mean to take a day off, to *rest,* to play. The Sabbath is a day of rest and play, of delight and praise.[31] In it we take our repose in a God who can be trusted and should be praised. It is the climax of creation, the perfect day. And by trusting God, praising God, and taking delight in the works of God, we refuse to reduce ourselves to makers and designers; we refuse to reduce our existence to joyless and incessant work; and we refuse to reduce the moral life to utility, to a concern about consequences. The future is chosen not just in the technology to construct some plastic destiny but already in the imagination, in the image of ourselves with which human creativity (or co-creativity) begins.[32] This *mythos* orients us not only to the val-

30. On "stewardship" see Appendix B.

31. See Norman Wirzba, *Living the Sabbath: Discovering the Rhythms of Rest and Delight* (Grand Rapids: Brazos, 2006).

32. Julian Hartt, *The Restless Quest* (Philadelphia: United Church Press, 1975), pp. 117-34.

ues we may hope to achieve but also — and fundamentally — to the values we display.

The story also suggests a third thing, of course, a thing seldom overlooked in these discussions. The story suggests that human creativity — or co-creativity — is given with the creation, that human beings are created and called to exercise *"dominion"* in the creation, "dominion" over nature. This was, of course, central to the complaint of Lynn White, Jr., who objected not only to the "disenchantment" of nature in Genesis 1 but also and especially to this notion of "dominion." We have already responded to White, arguing that his complaint is properly targeted not at the biblical story but at the use (or abuse) of the story beginning in the seventeenth century. Here we must give a more constructive account of "dominion." How can humanity reflect God's way in "dominion"? How can humanity make God's own rule manifest by its exercise of "dominion"?

Fortunately, the answer is not far. Already at the creation, God's own "dominion" is care. God calls the world into existence by his word, "Let there be. . . ." The jussive form, "Let there be . . . ," captures both God's dominion and God's care.[33] The jussive form is matched in each case by the declarative, "and there was. . . ." God summons the world into existence as a realm characterized by a fertile and free otherness to God and commits himself to it. God blesses the world and all its creatures, completing and affirming its fertile and free otherness. Such is the context for the blessing on humankind and its "dominion." To use a contrast that Jesus made (Mark 10:45-46), God's ruling is not like that of Gentile rulers, those

33. See Oliver Davies, *A Theology of Compassion: Metaphysics of Difference and the Renewal of Tradition* (London: SCM Press, 2001), p. 267.

tyrants who "lord it over" their subjects. And it is not to be so among those who would image God. Those who would exercise dominion must be servants. This is not to disown power or "dominion," but it is to construe it as service to God and to the neighbor and to the creation. Dominion is exercised in care, in blessing the creation, in affirming God's good gifts. The human effort to understand nature and to exercise "dominion," in principle, at least, fits the story Christians tell, but the story sets "dominion" in the context of the human response — and responsibility — to the God who delights in and cares for the creation.

If instead of turning back to God's creative act to consider "dominion" we look ahead to the second (and older) account of creation in Genesis 2:4b-25 (also not far), we hear that God put Adam, who had been formed "from the dust of the ground [*adamah*]" (2:7), in the garden "to till it and to keep it" (2:15). My colleague Ellen Davis has observed that the word translated "to till" *('avad)* is the ordinary verb for "work" and that it normally means "to work for" someone. It might mean, therefore, that Adam is set in the garden to "work for the land." It can also mean, however, what we ordinarily take it to mean, that Adam is "to work the land." We might simply set the point aside as another indication of the problem of the difficulty of translating Scripture, but then she makes the quite stunning observation that "to keep" *(shamar)* is almost a technical term for "keeping" the law or God's ordinances.[34] To "keep" the land does not mean to exercise ownership rights over it; it means to "observe" the land, to have an attitude toward it that at least resembles the

34. Ellen Davis, *Getting Involved with God: Rediscovering the Old Testament* (Cambridge, MA: Cowley, 2001), pp. 191-95.

attitude of the pious Jew toward the law. *Shamar* is used repeatedly in Psalm 119, for example, and in connection with the deference to and delight in the law that characterizes that meditation on the law. To "keep" the land requires something like the same deference and delight. And God "keeps," that is to say, he "guards," "cares for," and "blesses" (e.g., Ps. 121 and the Aaronic blessing, Num. 6:24-26). The human vocation to image God's care, to be a sign of God's own rule, includes "dominion," but the meaning of "dominion" is not far from God's "keeping," from protection and care and blessing. It is to God, after all, that we are responsible in our responsibilities for nature and altering it.

There are additional clues in the creation narratives about our vocation to be a sign of God's own rule in the creation. We image God *as relational beings.* The God who made us is the triune God, whose own life is a story of communal and eternal self-giving, and God made us social. God made us in and for relationships. The climactic sign of it in the creation story, of course, was that when God made humankind in God's own image, "male and female he created them" (Gen. 1:27). And the story makes clear that we are also in relationship with God — and no less clear that God set us in the context of — and in relationship with — the rest of the creation too. There is wisdom here when the project of liberal society would teach us to regard ourselves simply as autonomous individuals and our relationships simply as freely entered contracts. Our relationships with each other are not to be reduced to a set of contractual relationships between autonomous agents, and our interdependent relationship with nature may not be denied simply because there is no freely entered contract. We image God in self-giving, in practices of caring for and affirming the existence of the other, including the non-human other. The story orients us to respect for other human beings and respect for other beings as relational creatures. It orients us toward respect for natural relationships, including those human relationships that are not of our choosing but that are nevertheless constitutive of our human being and for our human vocation.[35]

And if the fourth clue was that God made us relational beings, the fifth is that God made us *embodied selves.* We image God as embodied selves. The second (but older) creation story in Genesis says that by God's breath and gift, the dust was made *nephesh,* "a living being" (Gen. 2:7). And precisely as *nephesh,* as living beings, human beings are "flesh," *basar.* There is no place here for a dualism that separates body and soul as though they were two things and not one whole, no place for a dualism that tempts us to think of redemption as deliverance *from* this world and *from* these bodies rather than as God's renewal *of* this world and *of* these bodies.

Whole selves, embodied selves, are "flesh" in their contrast to God and in their dependence upon God. The quite remarkable human powers to "have dominion" and to choose, are no less "flesh" than our bodies are. Those powers are not divine; in them, too, we may and must rely on God. We are our "flesh" in our creatureliness, in our finitude, weakness, and mortality. Human mortality, I think, is simply given with the creation, the simple sign that we do not have our life the way God has life, that we are dependent upon God for life itself. Before the fall, however, when distrust did not yet mark the relation of human beings to God, human mortality was ac-

35. That orientation has implications for a faithful discernment of the powers to alter the natural processes of begetting and much else, implications that we once again must leave to one side. See *Reading the Bible in the Strange World of Medicine,* pp. 253-393.

companied by confidence in God's power to give life even to the dust. After the fall, death would be joined to distrust and to the threat of alienation from our bodies, from our communities, and from God.[36]

The *nephesh*, "the living being," is *basar*, is "flesh." And without God human weakness and mortality would make their inevitable way toward death. Without God great human powers would demonstrate their weakness, their "flesh," by their inability to preserve the cosmos from tilting back to chaos. But in the creation and in the continuing creation the *basar*, the "flesh," is *nephesh;* it is *not* without God. The flesh, too, is from God, and it is good. The flesh is created by God to be with God. Whole selves, embodied selves, mortal and dependent, creative and powerfully gifted with reason and will, are flesh, and it is good. Human weakness and mortality find their answer, the answer to their longing, in God. And the human powers that are no less "flesh" find their vocation in God's project of blessing the whole creation. This human weakness and dependence would only be bad if the *nephesh* were without God — or if God were not dependable — or if, by some inexplicable fault, human beings in their anxiety about this vulnerability failed to depend on God. The inexplicable happened, of course, but more of that later.

For now, notice that there is wisdom here when genetic reductionism tempts us to reduce our selves to our genes and when the Baconian project tempts us to regard nature — including our own nature — as an enemy to be mastered. The story of our creation as embodied selves does not fit any re-

---

36. See Allen Verhey, "Science at the End of Life: Contributions and Limitations," *The Princeton Seminary Bulletin* 28, no. 1, new series (2007): 14-47.

duction of the self to mere body, to biological organism, or to the human genome. And neither does it fit divorcing the self from the body, and from the genome, as though that were simply an object and as though the self were simply identified with some "soul," with some ghost in the machine, or to the capacities for reason and choice and "dominion" that transcend the body. The story orients us to attend to whole selves. We may not reduce a human being, whether ourselves or another, either to objectified nature or to simple transcendence over it.[37]

Having mentioned our creation as male and female and our embodiment, a sixth clue is not hard to find. The Creator God has no gender, but God made us "male and female" and called us to be a sign of God's own rule also in this aspect of our sociality, our *sexuality.* Sex is good in the creation, very good. The vulnerability of nakedness was an occasion for delight, not shame. (That came with the fall [contrast Gen. 2:25 and Gen. 3:7]). And the delight was marked by mutuality, not power and patriarchy. (That, too, came with the fall [Gen. 3:16]).[38] This sexual delight and mutuality found expression already in the creation story in marriage, in a "one flesh" union in which promises of fidelity were implicit (Gen. 2:24; Mark 10:7-8). And already in the creation story this "one flesh" union contains the promise of the blessing of fruitful-

37. This orientation has implications, of course, for altering nature in the art of medicine, implications that again we leave to one side. See Allen Verhey, *Reading the Bible in the Strange World of Medicine,* pp. 68-98.

38. The creation of woman as "helper" (2:18) does not mark the woman as subordinate to the man; God is also called a "helper," after all. Against the patterns of patriarchy, in which a woman leaves the house of her parents to join the house of her husband, in Genesis 2:24 the pattern is "a man leaves his father and mother and cleaves to this wife."

ness, of children (Gen. 1:28).[39] Good sex "in the beginning" involved delight and mutuality, intimacy and continuity, and the blessing of children. Sex is good, but it is not God; nothing God made is God. From the beginning the story cautions against idolatrously extravagant expectations of either sexuality or procreation. When human fulfillment is made dependent on sexual fulfillment or on the fulfillment of procreative desires, then we have failed to remember the creation.

And from the beginning the story cautions against the dualism that drives a wedge between body and soul. This is a story of an embodied relationship, neither simply contractual nor

---

39. To be sure, the first record of a birth in Scripture (Gen. 4:1) comes hard on the heels of the fall and the curse (Gen. 4:1), but it comes as a sign that sin and the curse will not have the last word in God's world, a sign that God has not abandoned his project of blessing, and a sign of hope in a fallen world. The blessing of children — and the summons to "be fruitful and multiply" (Gen. 1:22) — calls for further commentary. The first comment is that things have changed. One thing that has changed, of course, is the world's population. It might well be argued that humankind has fulfilled the summons to "fill the earth" (Gen. 1:22). And if that is the case, then the story, I think, hardly prohibits couples from limiting the number of their children. But that is not the only change. Again things change with sin and the fall. The promise of children goes unfulfilled in the barrenness of Sarah and Rachel, for example. Infertility, too, like shame and patriarchy, comes after sin and the fall, and it is not regarded as "the good creation" of God, however "natural" it may seem. There is nothing in the creation story, I think, that would prohibit those for whom infertility seems a "given" from intervening in the "natural" process of procreation in order to have a child. Things change again with the coming of Jesus. Then the child of promise has been born, and born to all of us. After Jesus neither marriage nor childbearing are regarded as duties of Torah or of our status as God's creatures. Some things, however, have not changed. Children remain a blessing of God — and begetting them in a world like this one still properly remains a witness that God can be trusted. See further Allen Verhey, *Reading the Bible in the Strange World of Medicine,* pp. 253-303.

simply biological. As the story of our embodiment prompts a refusal to reduce the self either to mere physiology or to disembodied capacities for choice and contracts, so the story of our embodied sexuality prompts both a refusal to reduce "love-making" to pleasure-seeking without the commitments of fidelity (however "natural" it may seem) and a refusal to reduce "baby-making" to a technology of reproduction, to mere physiology (accompanied perhaps by a contract), without the commitment to care for children. The story has prompted the claim that both love-making and baby-making belong in the context of the commitments of marriage.

We do not signal God's rule by doing what comes "naturally" but by obedience to the summons of God the Creator, not by obedience to "the call of nature" but by obedience to the call of God. It is not "nature" that is normative but the God who is the Creator and the destiny of the creation. We signal God's rule in self-giving commitments of fidelity to our sexual partners and in caring for our children — even when they do not turn out quite as we expected. We may learn parenting from the one we learn in the story to call "Abba." There is wisdom here when a project of making perfect children tempts us to a different view of parenting. Parenting involves the uncalculating commitment to nurture, and we must orient ourselves to affirm practices of parenting that fit with such uncalculating nurture.[40]

---

40. Again there are implications for our altering of natural processes of begetting. It is not "nature" or the natural processes themselves that are normative but the cause of God. For example, practices of prenatal diagnosis with a view to abortion may put that parental commitment of uncalculating nurture at risk. Already we can diagnose a number of genetic conditions in a fetus, and the number is constantly growing. For most of these there is no therapy. The tests allow parents to make a decision about

There is a final clue in the creation stories. God made us *free.* God is the sovereign Creator, but God's creation proceeds by the sharing of power. The earth, for example, is invited to bring forth vegetation, and it does. God is not the only agent in the story. The whole creation responds to the creative activity of God. The agency of the creature is the result of God's action, but it is invited to its own action in response and praise.

The sovereign Creator God is also the source and destiny of human freedom. The story of creation in Genesis 1 stood in

---

whether to give birth or to abort. How shall we "image" God here? How shall we act in ways that are responsible to God? If God's cause is life rather than death, then those who would "image God" will not be disposed to abort; they will not celebrate abortion as a "therapeutic option." There are, I think, genetic conditions that justify abortion. Something like the same conditions that would prompt nurturing parents to remove a child from life-support may, I think, justify removing them from the life-support of the womb. There are conditions like Tay-Sachs that consign a child not only to an abbreviated life but to a life subjectively indistinguishable from torture. And there are conditions like Trisomy 18 that are inconsistent not only with life but with the minimal conditions for human communication. Pre-natal diagnosis — and abortion — can be used responsibly. However, when some children with Down's Syndrome are aborted because they have Down's, there seems to exist a reasonable possibility that prenatal diagnoses have been — and will be — used irresponsibly. And when some girls are aborted because they are girls, it seems obvious that the tests have been — and will be — used irresponsibly. When the slogan about "preventing birth defects" is taken to justify preventing the birth of "defectives," those who do not measure up to the standards or match the preferences of parents, then there are reasons to worry a little, to worry that the disposition of a good "parent" will change from the sort of uncalculating nurture that can evoke and sustain trust from children to the sort of calculating nurture that is prepared to abandon or abort the offspring who do not match specifications. To image God would sustain care for the weak and the helpless, and for the little ones who do not measure up. On abortion see further *Reading the Bible in the Strange World of Medicine,* pp. 194-252.

polemical relation to the story the Babylonians told. Humanity was not created from the blood of an evil god to be a servant to the gods and to Babylon but to be free. And the power of God at the creation is not unrelated to the power of God to liberate some slaves from Egyptian bondage or some exiles from Babylon.[41] Human freedom was — and is — a gift of God. It is the good gift of God by which God would form humanity for voluntary fellowship with God and with each other and for the care and tending of the creation. That alone should prevent the determinism of genetic reductionism. Respect for a human being as the "image of God" is not exhausted by respect for the freedom of a human being, but it surely includes it. Freedom is a prerequisite for the moral life, but the moral life should not be reduced to it, and it can be deformed. The solution for our world is not simply to maximize freedom, as in the project of liberal society. But neither can the solution be simply to eliminate freedom. It is still the gift of God, and by that gift we are not simply fated by our past arrogance toward nature to continue it. We are freed to respond to God and to the cause of God by blessing the creation, by turning from the abuse of the creation to delight in it and care for it. To be sure, we frequently fail to be faithful in our freedom, but God continues to summon us, and in summoning us grants us freedom. The story itself summons us to faith and faithfulness, frees us for a renewed relation with the creation, even while it orients us also toward respect for human beings and human freedom.[42]

41. See especially Isaiah 51:9-16 and 45:12-13.
42. To attempt to coerce faith violates the freedom God gives. The freedom that God gives and that demands our respect, it should be noted, is not simply the ability arbitrarily to will one thing one moment and the contrary thing the next, but the freedom to establish a self and then to live with integrity.

2. . . . but Sin

Creation, of course, is not the whole of the story. The story continues, and the plot thickens, with the story of *human sin*. While Scripture says, and says plainly, that "in the beginning" God makes all things and makes all things good, it knows as well that there is something wrong with our world.[43] There is a flaw, a fault, that runs through our world and through our lives and through our selves. To make our way through the world and through life evokes not only senses of dependence and gratitude but also a sense of remorse. It is an inexplicable mystery, but this much is clear in Scripture: The fault that runs through our world is not God's fault — and, in spite of the Baconian project, it is not the fault of nature either. The fault is ours.

The fault is traced to human sin, to the human refusal to trust God and to give thanks to God. "Claiming to be wise, they became fools; and they exchanged the glory of the immortal God for [idols]" (Rom. 1:22-23). Grasping at freedom in the demand to be autonomous and a law to themselves, they found themselves in bondage, in that "voluntary bondage" to the powers of sin and death that usurp God's rule and resist God's cause. Scripture continues with the story of hu-

---

43. The story of Scripture does not deny the reality and power of evil. On the contrary it confirms it. The Priestly story of creation never says that there is no evil in the world. Exiles in Babylon would hardly deny it. Nevertheless, it tells a story in which God makes all things and makes all things good. The Babylonian epic needed no story of the fall, but the Jewish exiles did. And they had one. The older story of creation (the Yahwist account, Gen. 2:4b-25) continued with the story of human failure and of a curse (Gen. 3:1-24). Evil is in no sense the first word about nature, nor, as we shall see, the last word.

man sin and of the curse that followed in its train. That "curse" involved the alienation of human beings from each other, from God, and from the creation itself.

As we have already observed, the seventeenth-century reading of the Genesis story attended to a feature of the story that subsequent centuries (and what we have called the Baconian project) too often overlooked. According to Bacon, the fall and the curse that came in its wake left its mark not only on humanity but also on the rest of nature. As a result of human sin "the ground" was cursed (Gen. 3:17); the natural world was affected by human sin. The image of a nature that has fallen into ruin on account of human transgressions seems at least as appropriate for late modernity as it was for the ancient period or the seventeenth century. And the vocation to care for nature, burdened by our own fault, is even more pressing than when John Donne insisted "our business is, to rectify nature, to what she was."[44] Our "altering nature" should be accompanied by repentance for the human attitudes and actions that have despoiled it — and oriented toward forms of recompense, toward something like restoration ecology. We should be more attentive to the ways our efforts to master nature have led to nature's woe and more intentional about intervening to initiate or accelerate an ecosystem's recovery.[45]

Still, we should be careful here, a little suspicious of Bacon's account of nature as "cursed" and "fallen." If we begin by presupposing that the goodness of the creation is inconsis-

44. John Donne, "To Sir Edward Herbert at Julyers," in *Donne* (New York: Dell, 1962), p. 103.

45. See the Society for Ecological Restoration and Policy Working Group, "The SER Primer on Ecological Restoration, Version 2," http://www.ser.org/reading_resources.asp.

tent with what is called "natural evil," inconsistent with death or predation, then the conclusion seems unavoidable that nature itself is "fallen." We have, however, already denied that premise, and here we would worry a little over that conclusion. The worry is prompted in part by the confusion of two senses of nature, nature as the creation (nature #5, everything but God)[46] and nature in contrast to humanity (nature #10, everything but humanity).[47] To claim that nature (#10) is "fallen" can tempt us to identify nature as the enemy and technology as the faithful savior. That was the temptation into which the heirs of Bacon fell. And if nature is "cursed," then another inference is also possible even if Bacon and Donne would have rejected it. If nature is cursed, look to another world. If nature is cursed, then damn it all.

But that is not the biblical story, and those are not biblical inferences. In the biblical story, nature (#5, the creation) continues to give its mysterious and sinless obedience to the Creator. It is not cursed but cared for by God. To be sure, the story is that the ground was "cursed," but not because nature had sinned or failed to obey the summons of God. "Cursed is the ground *because of you*" (Gen. 3:17, italics added). It is human sin, not some fault in nature, that is at the root of the curse. And to be sure, there is a mysterious solidarity and interdependence between *Adam* and the ground *(adamah)* from which he was made and to which he will return. That solidarity and interdependence are also reflected in the curse upon the ground following human sin. That sin alienated Adam from *adamah,* rendered the relationship dysfunctional. The

46. Or, to leave open the question of the fall of angelic powers, nature #6, everything "under the moon."

47. Or, to reflect Cartesian dualism, nature #11, everything but human capacities for knowledge and choice.

remedy is not to regard nature as the enemy or technology as the savior. And the remedy is not to regard nature as god and technology as the enemy. The remedy is the summons of God to live as signs of God's own care for God's creatures. We should be as obedient to that summons as the sun is in its rising. Scripture never construes nature either as guilty or as intrinsically corrupt; it never condemns nature.

To return to the topic of human sin, we might profitably consider Reinhold Niebuhr, the twentieth-century theologian who retrieved the doctrine of sin as an antidote for the optimistic liberalism of the nineteenth and early twentieth century. Following Kierkegaard, the nineteenth-century Danish thinker who is often called "the father of existentialism," Niebuhr tried to explain the inexplicable in the anxiety that attends the fact that we are simultaneously finite and free. Human beings are always at once the finite children of nature and free children of spirit, and we are always tempted to deny one or the other, to deny our finitude in *pride* or to deny our transcendence of nature in sensuality and *sloth*.[48] Pride and sloth have a variety of forms, of course, but they still promise, or threaten, to orient our human projects, including our projects of altering nature. Pride is at work whenever we would attempt to eliminate our anxiety by eliminating the vulnerabil-

48. Reinhold Niebuhr, *Nature and Destiny of Man: A Christian Interpretation* (Louisville: Westminster/John Knox Press, 1996). See further Mark J. Hanson, "Indulging Anxiety: Human Enhancement from a Protestant Perspective," in *Christian Bioethics* 5, no. 2 (1999): 121-38; Jean Bethke Elshtain, *Who Are We? Critical Reflections and Hopeful Possibilities* (Grand Rapids: Eerdmans, 2000), pp. 39-80 on the "prideful self," pp. 81-126 on the "slothful self"; and Lisa Sowle Cahill, "Cloning and Sin: A Niebuhrian Analysis and a Catholic, Liberationist Response," in Ronald Cole-Turner, ed., *Beyond Cloning: Religion and the Remaking of Humanity* (Harrisburg, PA: Trinity Press International, 2001), pp. 97-110.

ity that attends our finitude; it is at work in the promises of genetic technology that identify the fault in our world with our finitude and would attempt to provide a technological remedy for it. Sloth is at work whenever we would deny our freedom in an effort to escape responsibility;[49] it is at work in genetic research whenever we accept genetic reductionism and determinism. No map that would orient us to nature and to altering it would be complete without attention to human pride and sloth.

That we are made both finite and free is a call to faith and faithfulness, not a license to pride or sloth. Sin entered the story in the serpent's intimation that God is a liar and not to be trusted. It is important to say again that the problem with Adam's world — with our world — is not finitude. Finitude is good, intended to be the occasion of trust. In finitude, with its limits and dependency, we may learn that God and the neighbor are to be trusted. And it is important to say again that the problem with Adam's world — with our world — is not free-

---

49. Elshtain, *Who Are We?*, pp. 88-89, regards certain "current projects of self-overcoming," including the Human Genome Project, as "examples of denials of finitude as a form of slothfulness, indolence where cultural demands and trumpeted enthusiasms are concerned. These projects are tricky to get at because they present themselves to us in the dominant language of our culture — choice, consent, control — and because they promise an escape from the human condition into a realm of near mastery. We are readily beguiled with the promise of a new self. In so doing, we may deny or harm the only self we have. . . . As we seek cures for the human condition, the desperate edge of that seeking bespeaks a conviction that our imperfect embodiment *is* the problem that must be overcome. For example: a premise — and promise — driving the Human Genome Project, the massive effort underway to map the genetic code of the entire human race, is that we might one day intervene decisively in order to guarantee better if not perfect human products."

dom. Freedom is a good gift of God the creator, part of the cause of God the redeemer; it is prerequisite to our human response-ability and to a voluntary fellowship of gracious giving and receiving. Both pride and sloth are folly.

There is wisdom here when the project of liberal society would take freedom to be a sufficient moral principle. Certainly persons must respect others, and that surely entails that they must respect the capacities for agency in other persons. But persons are always more than their rational autonomy, and we must not allow the principle of respect for persons to be reduced to respect for their autonomy. Persons must also regard others and respect others as embodied persons. We must regard and respect others not only as free individuals but also as "members one of another," as members of communities at least some of which are not of their own choosing. We must regard and respect others also as mysteriously related in solidarity and interdependence with nature. And we must regard and respect not only human persons but the creation itself.

3. God Comes Again to Covenant and to Bless

Sin, however, is not the end of the story either. And neither is the curse. And neither is the flood. The story of the flood (Gen. 6–9) is a story of judgment, of course, a story of God's resolve to destroy humanity and the earth because of "the wickedness of humankind" (6:5) and because "the earth was filled with violence" (6:11). But it is also a story of grace, and of grace not only on Noah but also upon the earth and its creatures. "Noah found favor in the sight of the Lord" (6:8), and God told Noah to build an ark and to gather male and female of all the creatures of the earth into it (6:19). Then the waters came, but Noah and his menagerie were saved. Once more, in a new beginning, God made a wind to blow over the earth (8:1; cf. Gen. 1:2), and the waters of chaos no longer threatened. Once more, in a new beginning, the animals made their way upon the earth to "be fruitful and multiply" (8:17; cf. Gen. 1:22). But now God makes a covenant, a covenant with Noah and his descendants, to be sure, but it is more strikingly also a covenant with "every living creature" (9:10, 12, 15, 16), with "all flesh that is on the earth" (17), indeed, with "the earth itself" (13), with nature. It is "an ecological covenant."[50] And this "ecological covenant" is an "everlasting covenant" (16). God makes covenant with humanity and with the creation, promising not to destroy the creation, promising protection of "endangered species." We are part of that covenant as part of nature and as caretakers of nature, and our relation with both God and with the rest of the creation is henceforth covenantal.

The sign of this "ecological covenant" is the rainbow. A rainbow, any rainbow, may serve to remind humanity of God's care for the earth and its creatures. In the story, however, the rainbow serves to remind *God* of this covenant (9:15-17). Moreover, the bow is pointed at the heavens. The story is that God makes God vulnerable; when the creation is destroyed or abused, God suffers. God freely chooses to share the vulnerability of nature. God gives to Noah and his posterity a renewed charge of "dominion" which provides for the rule of law to resist the human tendency to violence and moral anarchy that prompted the judgment of the flood (9:1-7). God's self-limiting promise "never again" to destroy all living things — and God's accep-

---

50. Bernard Anderson, *From Creation to New Creation* (Minneapolis: Augsburg Fortress, 1994), p. 157.

tance of vulnerability — display a remarkable trust in Noah, in his character and in his capacities as guardian and caretaker of nature. Still, in the midst of the responsibilities to resist violence and to care for the creation his posterity should not forget God's vulnerability or neglect God's suffering.

The flood, of course, did not vanquish human sin. Sin asserted itself almost as soon as Noah and his family disembarked. It showed its power both in sloth and pride, in the context of drunken nakedness and in the context of great technological ambition at the Tower of Babel (Gen. 11). The curse still followed in the wake of sin. Against the hubris of the tower-builders, who would build a city and a tower "to make a name for [them]selves" and lest they "be scattered" (11:4), God confused their language. The people could not understand one another. They had to give up their project, and ironically they ended up "scattered" (11:9). The problem, it should be observed, was not that the project involved technology; the problem was pride. And the solution was not more or better technology or a romantic rejection of technology. The solution was humble obedience to the summons of God when God comes again to covenant and to bless. Hard on the heels of the disaster at Babel, God comes to Abraham and Sarah and calls them and their descendants to be a blessing to all the nations (Gen. 12:1-3). And that blessing finds expression in the agricultural skills of Isaac, in the horticultural skills of Jacob, and in the skills of Joseph as an administrator in a time of famine. All these technologies were a blessing to "the nations."[51] Technology can stand in the service of God's cause to

51. See Hans Walter Wolff, "The Kerygma of the Yahwist," in Walter Brueggemann and Hans Walter Wolff, *The Vitality of Old Testament Traditions* (Atlanta: John Knox, 1975), pp. 41-66.

protect the creation and to bless the nations. The problem, the fault, that runs though the story — and through our lives and our common life — is not located in either nature or in technology but in the human pride that would seize what must be received as God's gift and in the human sloth that refuses its response-ability to God.

The story of Abraham and his descendants continued, of course, and there is much in Hebrew Scripture that could reward attention when Christians think about nature and about altering it. Here we can give only hints and tokens.

The stories of creation and covenant oriented the statutes of the Torah to the care of both neighbor and nature. The commandment that there should be a Sabbath, for example, was not just a commandment that "you" should take a Sabbath and remember God's gifts but also that "you" should provide a Sabbath, a little rest, both for human creatures, for "your son or your daughter, your male or female slave, . . . or the alien resident," and for "your livestock" (Exod. 20:10; Deut. 5:14).[52] The law, moreover, also insisted on a Sabbath year for the land, a year of rest for the land (Lev. 25:3-5). And in the year of Jubilee, the year after the seventh sabbatical year, the fiftieth year, the land is to lie fallow again and those who have lost their land are restored to it. The premise of this practice is stated in Leviticus 25:23: the land belongs to God finally; it does not belong finally to any son or daughter of Abraham or Adam; they are but "aliens and tenants" with God on God's land. To give just one other example, the Torah commands attention to nature; not even war allows the abuse of nature; "If you besiege a town . . .

52. The version in Exodus recalls the creation story. The version in Deuteronomy 5:12-15 recalls the exodus and God's deliverance from slavery in Egypt.

you must not destroy its trees by wielding an ax against them. Although you may take food from them you must not cut them down" (Deut. 20:19).[53] Perhaps even more striking than the statutes themselves, however, is the triangulated relationship of God, the people, and the land,[54] reflecting the relationships of God, humanity, and nature established in the creation.

The prophets assumed that triangulated relationship. When Israel breaks covenant, then it is not just God and Israel that suffer but nature, too. As Hosea says, "the land mourns, and all who live in it languish; together with the wild animals and the birds of the air, even the fish of the sea" (Hos. 4:3). The same prophet envisioned a future in which God's steadfast, patient love would overwhelm human resistance, a future in which the covenant and blessing would encompass all the nations and all of nature (Hos. 2:14-23; cf. also Isa. 11:6-9; Ezek. 34:25-31). God's good future would evidently not be *God's* good future if it did not include the creation's flourishing.

The wisdom literature looked to nature as a moral teacher. The sages observed nature closely and called upon those who would be wise to "observe" its ways.

> Four things on earth are small,
>   yet they are exceedingly wise:
> the ants are a people without strength,
>   yet they provide their food in the summer;
> the badgers are a people without power,
>   yet they make their homes in the rocks;

---

53. Steven Bouma-Prediger, *For the Beauty of the Earth*, p. 149, comments perceptively on this and other verses, "We are permitted to use the fruit of the earth, but we are not allowed to destroy the earth's ability to be fruitful."

54. See Christopher J. H. Wright, *God's People in God's Land: Family, Land, and Property in the Old Testament* (Grand Rapids: Eerdmans, 1990), pp. 104-5.

the locusts have no king,
yet all of them march in rank;
the lizard can be grasped in the hand,
yet it is found in kings' palaces.

(Prov. 30:24-28)[55]

Indeed, according to Proverbs 8, when Lady Wisdom calls upon the fools to learn from her, she announces that she was present at the creation, the first of God's creatures, God's partner in the creation, "rejoicing in his inhabited world and delighting in the human race" (Prov. 8:31). The presence of Lady Wisdom at the creation seems to be the basis for her invitation, "And now, my children, listen to me; happy are those who keep my ways" (Prov. 8:32). To keep the ways of wisdom is to rejoice in the creation and to keep, "observe," its ways. We have already paid some brief attention to God's answer to Job (Job 38–41), but let anyone who foolishly fails to stand in awe and joy before the Creator and the works of the Creator read the passage again. It is like "spectacles" (to use Calvin's image) to correct our anthropocentric vision, to see God's rule in the wonderful diversity of the natural world more clearly, to see ourselves more humbly. Perhaps in response we may join the joyful song of the morning stars at the creation (Job 38:7).

Some of the psalms did join that joyful song. Many hymns praise God as the Creator, expressing gratitude or humility or joy or awe in the midst of God's creative work (e.g., Ps. 8; 19:1-6, 29; 33:1-3; 104; 145:16; 147; 148). The psalmists delighted in the creation and in the praise it renders to the Creator. But I hasten on to the center of the story that Christian Scripture tells.

---

55. My grandson Ryan tells me, however, that the ant is the strongest animal in the world relative to its size.

4. The Center of the Christian Story

There — at the center of the Christian Scriptures — is the story of Jesus of Nazareth. That story begins with the stories of his *birth*. The Gospels tell the stories of his birth, of course, long after that birth itself, after his ministry, after the cross and resurrection, after Pentecost and the birth of the church. It is not the center of the story of Jesus,[56] but after the resurrection, after God had vindicated the crucified Jesus as "both Lord and Messiah" (Acts 2:36), his birth was remembered and celebrated. It was there, as John said, that "the Word became flesh and dwelt among us" (John 1:14). The powerful and creative Word that had summoned creation into existence became flesh. The Word that spoke the human creature into being became a human creature. God made human nature his own. The Word became flesh, and it was good. The incarnation forever marks creation and the human creature, nature and human nature, as good.

He was "conceived . . . and born. . . ." What attitude toward little ones is fitting to such a story? One does not have to take the birth stories of Luke as an objective record in order to appreciate the fact that for the Gospel of Luke the personal history of Jesus of Nazareth begins in the womb. It is true that it can be told as the story of Jesus of Nazareth only after he is identifiable among us, only after he has a name. And it is true that the story was told after the light of resurrection had illumined the whole of his life, even the darkness of the womb. Even so, in the story the personal identity of Jesus (like the

---

56. Mark, for example, the earliest of the Gospels, does not tell a story of Jesus' birth. Nor do the sermons in Acts in which the disciples first proclaim the gospel by telling the story of Jesus (e.g., Acts 2:14-36).

body from which it is inseparable) reached from the womb to God's strength on the other side of the tomb. That alone should point us toward a high regard for and generous hospitality to nascent life in our altering nature.

To be sure, the story does not give a tidy set of criteria to decide who counts as a "person." This orientation toward hospitality to nascent life, however, may help us to discern who counts, may help us to see another as a person, as "someone who..." enters our life with possibilities of its own. At the very least it will make us a little suspicious of the question "Who counts as a person?" whenever it is used to discount the responsibilities of hospitality and care.[57]

There are stories of his *ministry.* He came announcing the good future of God and already making its power felt in his works of power and in his words of blessing. Consider, first, those works of power, his miracles. It is assumed frequently that a miracle is antithetical to nature, a violation of "natural laws." And there are many, including some theologians, who, because they assume "the causal nexus in space and time which Enlightenment science and philosophy introduced into the Western mind," no longer regard the stories of miracle as credible.[58] Others, among whom I count myself, have

---

57. The story of the Good Samaritan is relevant here. The Good Samaritan was a neighbor to the one left "half-dead" by the side of the road, and in that care he — and all who heard the parable — discovered an unexpected answer to the question, "Who is my neighbor?" (cf. Luke 10:29-37). See further Oliver O'Donovan, *Begotten or Made?* (Oxford: Clarendon, 1984), pp. 48-66; see also O'Donovan, "Again: Who Is a Person?," in J. H. Channer, ed., *Abortion and the Sanctity of Human Life* (Exeter: Paternoster Press, 1985), pp. 125-37; and Allen Verhey, *Reading the Bible in the Strange World of Medicine,* pp. 229-36.

58. So, for example, Langdon Gilkey, "Cosmology, Ontology, and the Travail of Biblical Language," in Owen C. Thomas, ed., *God's Activity in the*

insisted that the "causal nexus" is not "closed," that the regularities of the world we name as "natural laws" are not the regularities of a self-contained machine but rather simply the ways God ordinarily works. As God acted freely and purposefully in creating the world, bringing things into existence and endowing them with causal powers of their own, so God acts freely and purposefully in sustaining the creation, sustaining things and their powers of causation, concurring in their existence and in the exercise of their own powers, their fertile and free otherness. As Nick Wolterstorff has said, "Historically what lay behind calling them (i.e., regularities) 'laws' was the conviction that their holding is to be attributed to God's creating, sustaining, and concurring wisdom and power."[59]

A miracle manifests the "supernatural," to be sure, but much depends on the meaning of "supernatural." Up until the seventeenth century the word was used (and usually as an adverb) to describe some change in the powers of people and things beyond their "natural" powers, beyond the powers that they ordinarily displayed. So a farmer could fatten a pig to an extent that the pig would not have reached on its own; such a pig could then be said to be "supernaturally" fat, fat beyond its "nature." The theological use was fully consistent with that usage, describing some change in the powers of people or things wrought by God. If Balaam's ass speaks, he speaks "supernaturally," for it is surely beyond the ordinary powers of an ass to speak. If Scrooge acts generously, his generosity is "supernat-

---

World: The Contemporary Problem (Chico, CA: Scholars Press, 1983), p. 31. See also, for example, John Macquarrie, *Principles of Christian Theology,* 2nd ed. (New York: Scribner's, 1977), pp. 247-48.

59. Nicholas Wolterstorff, *Divine Discourse: Philosophical Reflections on the Claim That God Speaks* (Cambridge: Cambridge University Press, 1995), p. 127.

ural," beyond the ordinary powers of a miser and attributed finally to the grace of God at work. The one thing that would not
be, could not be, described as "supernatural" would be God.
That all changed in the seventeenth century. Then the "supernatural" (and usually as a noun) identifies a being or beings
outside of "nature" (nature #15). Then it is not Scrooge's generosity that is "supernatural" but the ghosts'. And, of course,
God is "supernatural." The change corrodes a biblical imagination. Suddenly "nature" is autonomous and independent of
God, a closed system of cause and effect, and God, if God exists
at all, exists in some "other" world.[60] But suppose, with the
biblical story, that God is the Creator and Sustainer of this
world, that God is at work in the ordinary regularities of our
lives — and in the extraordinary events that surpass our expectations. Then miracles are the grace and power of God at work,
not violating nature, but gracing it. As George MacDonald
said, "The miracles of Jesus were the ordinary works of His Father, wrought small and swift that we might take them in."[61]

The story is, at any rate, that Jesus performed miracles. And
in his miracles, the good future of God already made its power
felt. "The miracles of Jesus were all 'miracles of the kingdom,'
evidence that God's sovereignty was breaking in, with a new ef-
fectiveness, upon the confusion of a rebellious world."[62] Then
the miracles may be regarded not as violations of nature but as
the eschatological fulfillment, completion, and perfection of

60. See C. S. Lewis, *Studies in Words,* 2nd ed. (Cambridge: Cambridge
University Press, 1967), pp. 64-68, and Nicholas Lash, *The Beginning and
End of 'Religion'* (Cambridge: Cambridge University Press, 1996), p. 168.
61. George MacDonald, *The Cause of Spiritual Stupidity,* cited in C. S.
Lewis, *George MacDonald: An Anthology* (New York: Macmillan, 1962), p. 58.
62. G. B. Caird, cited in C. F. D. Moule, *Man and Nature in the New Testament* (London: Athlone Press, 1964), p. 17.

nature. In these works of power the creation itself is being made new, not violated. In these works of power the Word that was present at the creation summons nature to its own perfection.

Consider, for example, one of the so-called nature miracles, the stilling of the storm (Mark 4:35-41; Matt. 8:23-27; Luke 8:22-25). In the Old Testament the power of God to create and to sustain the creation is often associated with God's power to command the winds and to summon the seas to calm. At the creation, of course, God called the wind to move upon the waters (Gen. 1:2). In Psalm 107:23-30 those who "went down to the sea in ships" saw firsthand God's "wondrous works in the deep." At God's command the stormy wind "lifted up the waves of the sea." But God "made the storm be still, and the waves of the sea were hushed." In Psalm 89:9 God is praised, "You rule the raging of the sea; when its waves rise, you still them." (See also Ps. 29:3; 46:3; 93:3-4, and several other passages.) The disciples ask in the gospel story, "Who then is this, that even the wind and the sea obey him?" (Mark 4:41). But the answer is obvious enough to the reader, even if the disciples were simply filled with awe. This is the one who brings the intentions of God to fulfillment.

There is one further observation to be made concerning this story. It is, if you will, a story of Jesus' exorcism of the wind and the sea. It is, I think, no accident that the story stands alongside the story of the Gerasene demoniac. When Jesus "rebuked the wind, and said to the sea, 'Peace! Be still!'" (Mark 4:39), the reader may well remember the story of the exorcism in Mark 1:23-27, in which Jesus "rebuked [the demon], saying, 'Be silent'" (v. 25). An exorcism does not violate the human creature; it frees the human creature to be more truly itself. And the nature miracle does not violate nature; it brings nature to its own fulfillment.

It was concerning the exorcisms that Jesus said, "But if it is by the finger of God that I cast out the demons, then the kingdom of God has come upon you" (Luke 11:20). But wherever a miracle is performed, there the good future of God already makes its power felt. When the dead were raised, when the sick were healed, and when the seas were calmed, God's good future was already proleptically present and the cause of God displayed. That cause of God and that future rule of God must be manifested by human beings in their vocation as image of God.

The healing miracles of Jesus demonstrate that God's cause is life, not death, that God's cause is human flourishing, including the human flourishing we call health, not disease (however "natural" death and disease may be). And the nature miracles make it plain that God's cause is the blessing upon nature that calms the waters of chaos and restores nature itself to what God intends. God is not simply identified with natural processes, even if "nature" and natural processes are the way God ordinarily works; nor is God simply identified with the "miraculous" altering of nature, as if "nature" and natural processes were not the way God ordinarily works. There is warrant in the miracle stories, then, for "altering nature," but such a warrant includes the demand that "altering nature" serve the cause (or causes) of God.

Because the cause of God includes the human flourishing we call health, there is warrant for "altering nature" in the service of health. But for the same reason, there is also warrant for altering our environmental practices. To allow the environment to deteriorate is to allow threats to human health. The air we breathe, the water we drink, the toxins we ingest or come into contact with, all have effects upon our health. Preventive medicine and public health officials should be, and frequently are, at the forefront of concerns about the environment.

Because the cause of God includes the human flourishing we call health, there is warrant for "altering nature" in the service of health. But because the cause of God includes more and other goods than the human flourishing we call health (and because human flourishing itself includes more and other goods than health), lest we make "health" "a second god," we may not regard the warrant as a license to do anything or everything for the sake of health.[63]

Jesus was not only a healer, however; he was also one who preached good news to the poor. In Jesus God demonstrates again that God is one who takes the side of the poor. And if we find warrant in the miracles of Jesus to "alter nature" in service of health, we must also ask how any project to "alter nature" will affect the poor. We must be oriented toward a justice and a technology that fits good news to the poor. A justice that fits this story will not be confused with the moral minimalism of the project of liberal society; it is not the sort of tightfisted justice that simply wants to protect one's own interests from

63. There are implications here for the consideration of altering nature in medicine and in genetic research. There is, for example, much in genetic research to celebrate. We may celebrate, for example, the ability genetics gives us sometimes to decide which drug will work best with which patient, whether a common drug like codeine for pain relief, or a new drug like Herceptin in the treatment of breast cancer. We may surely celebrate the success of genetic therapy in some children born with severe combined immunodeficiency (SCID). See the very celebratory survey of some of the applications of the knowledge of the human genome in Kenneth W. Culver, "A Christian Physician at the Crossroads of New Genetic Technologies and the Needs of Patients," in Ronald Cole-Turner, *Beyond Cloning*, pp. 14-33. This orientation toward healing, however, is no license for any or every genetic intervention. The community formed by Scripture will need to exercise discernment. See further Verhey, *Reading the Bible in the Strange World of Medicine*.

the interference of a neighbor. A technology that fits this story will not simply adopt the myth of capitalism, trusting free markets to protect and bless the poor. To remember this story and to live it requires a concern for social justice that is especially attentive to the voices and needs of the poor. It will require that we be attentive not only to intriguing questions about the frontiers of technology and science but also to mundane questions about fairness. It will require questions about the fairness of the share the poor have — and are likely to have — in any project of "altering nature," in both the burdens and the benefits. It will require questions also about fairness, about burdens borne by the poor due to our abuse of the environment — and any effort to finally care for it.

Concerns about justice and about caring for the poor are frequently set in opposition to the concerns about the environment and caring for it. Endangered jobs are sometimes set in opposition to endangered species. To be sure, there are sometimes tragic decisions to be made, decisions to be made when evils gather and cannot all be avoided and when goods collide and cannot all be avoided. Such decisions call for patience and sacrifice, imagination and compromise. They call for consideration of ways to shift the burden of caring for the creation from the backs of the poor and for ways to shift the burden of caring for the poor from the poor earth. Without denying, then, that there are sometimes tragic decisions to be made, let it also be observed that justice for the poor and oppressed and care for the creation sometimes cohere quite closely. A notable 1987 study by the Racial Justice Commission of the United Church of Christ showed, rather interestingly, that the sites for dumping of toxic waste were mainly located in communities marked also by poverty and minority populations. Indeed, the two maps they produced of the United States, one showing toxic waste sites and the other showing areas of great concentrations of poverty and people of color, looked like the same map.[64]

Poor people and minority populations, once regarded as simply not very interested in environmental issues, should be and frequently are at the forefront of local concerns about the environment. In Durham, North Carolina, for example, where I live, the community organization DurhamCAN (Durham Congregations, Associations & Neighborhoods), a network of churches, synagogues, mosques, agencies that serve the poor, and neighborhoods, has called public attention to the pollution of Third Fork Creek, which runs near the McDougald Terrace public housing complex.

Jesus of Nazareth was a healer and one who preached good news to the poor, but the Gospels tie such stories of Jesus firmly to the story of the cross. Jesus "suffered under Pontius Pilate." He made the human cry of lament his own cry, "My God, my God, why have you forsaken me?"

There is no pretense in lament, no denial, no withdrawal to some otherworldly realities. There is no romantic effort to reduce the hurt to some domesticated account of nature. And there is no presumptuous claim to secure human wellbeing by the mastery of nature. The story of the cross provides a corrective both to the religious triumphalism that denies the sad-

---

64. Commission for Racial Justice, *Toxic Wastes and Race in the United States: A National Report on the Racial and Socioeconomic Characteristics of Communities with Hazardous Waste Sites* (New York: United Church of Christ, 1987). Vernice Miller-Travis, "Social Transformation through Environmental Justice," in Dieter T. Hessel and Rosemary Radford Ruether, eds., *Christianity and Ecology: Seeking the Well-Being of Earth and Humans* (Cambridge, MA: Center for the Study of World Religions, 2000), pp. 559-72, tells the story of this report. See also Richard Hofrichter, ed., *Toxic Struggles: The Theory and Practice of Environmental Justice* (Philadelphia: New Society Publishers, 1993).

ness of this world and to the technological triumphalism that presumes it can simply provide a technological remedy for it.

The story requires compassion of any who would follow this Jesus. But we must be careful here. We must be careful that we do not confuse an ancient virtue with its modern counterfeit. The ancient virtue fit the story of one who, God with us, made the human cry of lament his own cry. Modern compassion simply wants to stop the crying. Instead of being willing to suffer with another, modern compassion simply wants to put an end to suffering — and by any means necessary. The Baconian project has subverted compassion into trusting technology against suffering. Modern "compassion" simply and blindly arms itself with superior technique, relying not on wisdom but on artifice against suffering. Our enthusiasm for technology as a response to suffering has blinded us to the limits of technology.

The fault is not only or primarily in medicine or technology. When Christian communities forget lament, they marginalize not only suffering but also sufferers. When they leave aside lament in their liturgies, they nurture the expectation of invulnerability to suffering. Then in our anger or our sense of absurdity we think we sit alone in the congregation. So we reach for our bootstraps and struggle to lift ourselves to the heights of some triumphant liturgy, or else we reach for our technology and struggle to lift ourselves to invulnerability to suffering.

To remember and live the story of the cross would mean to recover the compassion that is ready *to suffer with* another human being and with the creation in its groaning, to share suffering, to respond with presence, not just tools, to arm compassion not only with artifice but with wisdom, not looking for technological solutions for what may not be technical problems.

The story is that God raised this Jesus up, that God vindicated this teacher and healer, this one who made the human cry of lament his own cry. And if "very good" was the first word of God over the creation, resurrection is the last word, and it rhymes with "very good." Jesus was raised in our world, in our history — in our nature — and our world, our history — the whole creation — has happily no escape. Creation is to be redeemed. To be sure, there will be transformations of the creation that surpass our imagination, but this much is clear from God's last word, already spoken at the resurrection of Christ: God does not destroy creation but renews it. God's last word over "space, time, and matter" will not be, "Oh well, nice try, good while it lasted but obviously gone bad, so let's drop it and go for a nonspatiotemporal, nonmaterial world instead."[65]

The early church struggled to find ways to express the significance of the resurrection, struggled to find language audacious enough, images deep and broad enough, to communicate its significance. Amid the great diversity of Christological images in the New Testament, consider just one, the image of the cosmic Christ.[66]

---

65. N. T. Wright, *Surprised by Hope: Rethinking Heaven, the Resurrection, and the Mission of the Church* (New York: HarperCollins, 2008), pp. 212-13.

66. Joseph Sittler, for whom the image of the "cosmic Christ" was at the heart of his "theology for nature," argued that, in spite of the plurality of images of Christ in the New Testament, "there clearly is a momentum and a directionality at work in the scope and variety of the New Testament witness to Jesus as the Christ," a momentum toward "widening circles of reference" until "all things" are encompassed in the work of Christ in Romans 8, Colossians 1, and Ephesians 1. See Sittler, "The Scope of Christological Reflection," *Interpretation* 26 (July 1972): 334. For a collection of Sittler's essays and for essays on his significance as a theologian for nature, see Steven Bouma-Prediger and Peter Bakken, *Evocations of Grace: The Writings of Joseph Sittler on Ecology, Theology, and Ethics* (Grand Rapids: Eerdmans, 2000).

In the language of the Christ Hymn in Colossians 1:15-20, Christ "is the image of the invisible God," the one in whom "all things in heaven and on earth were created," the one who was "before all things," and in whom "all things hold together," "the firstborn from the dead, so that he might come to have first place in everything," the one through whom "God was pleased to reconcile to himself all things." The work of Christ is cosmic in scope. Six times in the passage we hear of Christ and "all things."

Or consider Revelation 21:5 with its vision of Christ on the throne announcing, "See, I am making all things new." To be sure, "the first things have passed away" (Rev. 21:1, 4). Nothing less than a radical transformation is required, something like death and resurrection. There is surely judgment in Revelation, but it is not a judgment against the creation but against the bestiality of empire, against oppression, against "those who destroy the earth" (Rev. 11:18).[67] But although human beings may resist God and attempt to escape from God, God will not finally give his creation up to sin or death. God will have the last word over the creation, and the last word is that word of blessing, "all things" made new.

The claims are audacious indeed, but they are required by the identification of the Creator God and the Redeemer God and made plausible by the hilarious power and grace that raised Jesus from the dead. The Creator is the Redeemer; the Redeemer, the Creator. Redemption, then, is not the destruction of the creation but its renewal. And salvation is not to escape this world, this "nature," to some other world, but to

---

67. On Revelation see Barbara R. Rossing, "River of Life in God's New Jerusalem: An Eschatological Vision for Earth's Future," in Hessel and Ruether, eds., *Christianity and Ecology,* pp. 205-24.

have by God's grace a share in the renewal of the whole. And that salvation is already celebrated and displayed in worship and in the work both of protecting nature and of altering it in ways that anticipate God's good future.[68]

5. The End of the Story

God raised this Jesus up. The story is that the God of creation and covenant acted, as Jesus said he would, to end the rule of sin and death and to establish God's good future. Jesus was raised, and because he was, Christians hope for the renewal of "all things."

It is not yet that good future, of course — still sadly not yet that future. To hope for it, to hope for the redemption of "all things" and the renewal of "all things" is here and now to mourn, to ache, to lament that it is not yet. According to Paul in Romans 8 it is not just Christians who lament that this good future is not yet; "the creation waits with eager longing"

---

68. One may contrast such an eschatology, of course, with other forms of Christian eschatology that do envision the destruction of the world at the end of time. Where Christian eschatology posits an otherworldly mode of future existence, this world and nature may be regarded as ephemeral and unimportant. James Watt, Secretary of the Interior under President Reagan, famously defended the failure of his agency to protect the National Forests and Parks by saying, "I do not know how many future generations we can count on before the Lord returns" (quoted in Bouma-Prediger, *For the Beauty of the Earth*, p. 71). That such an eschatology is popular may be attested by the sales of books like Hal Lindsey's *The Late Great Planet Earth* and Tim LaHaye's *Left Behind* series. That such an eschatology is wrong may be attested exegetically and theologically. It remains critically important that Christianity work to get its own story straight, and N. T. Wright's *Surprised by Hope* helps considerably.

and "the whole creation has been groaning in labor pains until now" (Rom. 8:19, 22). Nature is no less responsive to God in the New Testament than in the Hebrew Scripture, still praising the Creator and waiting with an aching hope for the work of the Redeemer to have its full effect.

Human beings are called to respond as well, of course, to dream of a future in which God's creation can flourish, to mourn because it is not yet that future, and to act in response to that future so that it may make its power felt a little even now. With vision and lament and work, humanity — and the whole creation — can have some little taste of that future, even as we — and the whole creation — hunger and thirst for it.

That good future depends finally on God, not on us. We are not the Messiah; Jesus is. In the meanwhile, those who are given the vocation of the image of God may and must fulfill their responsibilities to God in nature — and in altering nature — not with the burden of messianic expectations but in carefree and joyful response to God's grace and future. And in the meanwhile, Christians should struggle to get their own story straight — and, of course, they should struggle to live it.

V

From Narrative to Practices, Prophecy, Wisdom, Analysis, and Policy

The struggle to live the story will engage the Christian community in practices that are performances of the story, but also in other forms of discourse besides narrative.[1] There will be a place for prophetic discourse, funded by the story. There will be a place for sage discourse, funded by prudence. There will be a place for analytical discourse as we try to get clear about our words, not just "nature" but "justice" and "responsibility" and a host of others. And there will surely be a place for policy discourse, for the art of the possible in the midst of the complexities presented by scientific and technological uncertainties, by economic and political realities, and by the inequalities that mark both national life and international relations. Narrative discourse is not sufficient for Christian ethics, but in all these other forms of discourse the story must not be forgotten.

---

1. James M. Gustafson developed these "forms of moral discourse" in his Stob Lectures, *Varieties of Moral Discourse: Prophetic, Narrative, Ethical, and Policy* (Grand Rapids: Calvin College and Seminary, 1988).

I have said little in these other forms of discourse. That was not because there is little to be said. On the contrary! But I have attended mainly to narrative because I am convinced that the biggest danger for the Christian community is forgetfulness. When we forget our story we suffer amnesia; we lose both our identity and our way. If we remember the story, we may respond again with gladness and with obedience, respond again to the God who creates and renews "all things," even us.

Still, as already said, narrative is not sufficient. The narrative does not tell us what to do here and now. The sabbatical year for the land is part of the story, but it is not part of a code about how to live the story in our time and place. It has authority as part of the story, not as a timeless rule. Faithful performance of the story today will require creativity as well as fidelity. Even so, the story remains fundamental to our identity and normative for our discernment. It provides the *mythos* that still forms an *ethos*. It provides a map that locates us in this creation and orients us within it. As the story tells us something of the work and cause of God, we discover something of the proper orientation of our life in response to God.

We have seen that the story calls us to turn from idols, to relate to God alone as God and to all other things as all other things are related to God. And we have seen that God's relation to the creation is care and covenant. We have seen that the story calls us to affirm the good creation of God, that it calls human beings to responsibility within the creation — to care for it, to delight in it, to know it in ways that are not simply mastery over it. We have seen that human "dominion" is not a license for arrogance, for "lording it over" nature, but a vocation to display God's rule and care in the midst of the creation. That vocation and the story itself orient us toward respect for the creation and its creatures, including the human creatures. Indeed, as human beings have a special responsibility to care for the whole of the creation as "image of God," they warrant a special respect within it. The respect due the human creature includes respect for their freedom, but it may not be reduced to that. It includes respect for human beings as relational, as constituted by relationships, some of which are not of their own choosing, including their intimate relationship with nature. And it includes respect for human beings as embodied, as finite and mortal creatures, dependent upon God and upon the good creation of God. The story of human sin evokes a sense of remorse, orients us to forms of recompense, both to the creation and to the persons we have wronged. It warns against the pride of our Promethean confidence in technology and against the sloth of neglecting our responsibility to God for God's creation and for those who need our care. The story reminds us that the problem with our world is neither nature nor technology but human pride and sloth. The story of Jesus orients us toward God's good future, toward the promise of *shalom* — to a day when humanity will be reconciled with both God and creation, when all things will be restored and peaceable difference will be the rule. The story calls us to words and works that already display that future, that already give some little token of it. It calls us to words and works of blessing the creation and the human creature, words and works of healing and other forms of "altering" nature that serve God's cause of blessing. It calls us to words and works that already display "good news for the poor," to a justice and a technology that fit such blessing. In the story of Jesus' suffering we saw a calling to compassion and to arm compassion not only with technology but with wisdom. And in the notion of the cosmic Christ we found a reminder that the Creator is the Redeemer and the Redeemer, the Creator. Redemption is not the destruction of the creation but its renewal. And salvation is not to escape this world, this "nature," but to have by God's grace a share in the renewal of the whole.

We did not find in the story, however, some simple code to govern our choices. And while we wait and watch and pray for God's good future, there is inevitably ambiguity. After all, one thing we have surely discovered about the cause of God is that it cannot be reduced to one simple thing. The cause of God is complex and various. It would be better to say, perhaps, that we find our orientation as we discover something of the causes of God. But if that is true, then our orientation, too, is complex and various. Perhaps it would be best to say that we find our orientations as we discover something of the causes of God. And those orientations do not always point in the same direction for our actions. Sometimes part of what we know about the cause of God seems to conflict with another part of what we know to be the cause of God. We have called attention, for example, to the tension that can sometimes exist between care for the creation and care for the poor. We do not escape moral ambiguity by remembering the story. Ambiguity is part of the moral life while we wait and watch and pray for the end of the story. Then there will be *shalom* also among the goods that belong to God's cause. Here and now, however, sometimes goods conflict and cannot all be chosen. Here and now, sometimes evils gather and cannot all be avoided. Still, the story gives us guidance as we think about our practices, our prophets, our prudence, and our politics.

Practices

If we remember the story, we may be prompted to change some of our habits, our practices, or to start some new ones. We might, for example, visit the farmer's market, buying food from local farmers instead of the food shipped thousands of miles. We might even start a little garden of our own, delighting in its flowers and in its food and being fairly regularly reminded that we need to better care for the soil.[2] We might plant more trees and use native plants. We might use less, living simply, and would surely recycle the things we do use. None of these practices will "save the planet," but they are a faithful response to God the Creator and both express and nurture care for the creation. And without such practices, it is unlikely that we will attend very carefully to policy.

There are also practices of the church to which we might give more attention. There is the practice, for example, of thanksgiving for the harvest. In many urban churches, if there remains such a practice at all, the prayers of thanksgiving seem curiously alien, a farmer's prayer rather than their own. But city-dwellers are no less dependent upon the land and its fertility than the farmer, even if less immediately dependent. If we were to sing harvest songs, we might be better equipped for delight and gratitude.

Your Spirit, O Lord, makes life to abound.
The earth is renewed, and fruitful the ground.

2. Many have made such a suggestion, but see especially Daniel Deffenbaugh, *Learning the Language of the Fields: Tilling and Keeping as Christian Vocation* (Cambridge, MA: Cowley, 2006), especially pp. 180-94.

To God be all glory and wisdom and might.
May God in his creatures forever delight.[3]

But it is not just at harvest time that the practices of the church can instill in us gratitude to God and care for the creation. In sermon and in church education there can be, sometimes is, and surely should be attention given to God's creation. When the table of the Lord is prepared with the offerings of the congregation, many churches practice both giving alms for the poor and remembering that the bread and wine come from the earth and from God's gracious provision. And however differently different Christian traditions account for it, there is a common recognition that the bread and wine, these things of nature, mysteriously participate in God's presence and in our praise.[4]

The churches, too, might change certain practices. For example, the practice of many megachurches to keep a manicured lawn might give way to a practice of sustaining native prairie grasses or to the practice of a communal garden. The money saved or the extra food might be used to care for the poor. Church buildings themselves might be constructed or remodeled in ways that are more energy efficient. Christian churches should display something of God's care for both the creation and the poor.

---

3. "Your Spirit, O Lord, Makes Life to Abound," *Psalter Hymnal* (Grand Rapids: CRC Publications, 1987), #104. The song, based on Psalm 104, continues in praise of the Creator and in delight in the creation.

4. See further Ben Quash, "Offering: Treasuring the Creation," in Stanley Hauerwas and Samuel Wells, eds., *The Blackwell Companion to Christian Ethics* (Oxford: Blackwell, 2004), pp. 306-18.

Prophets

The story funds not only practices but also prophetic voices. The Hebrew prophets regularly called attention to violations of covenant. They reiterated the claims of covenant. We are accustomed to think of the prophets as those who spoke God's word of judgment against those who abuse the poor — and properly so. But the "ecological covenant" signed by every rainbow has also been violated, and the story should embolden some to speak a word of judgment against those who abuse the earth or its creatures.

The prophets reminded those with power and privilege, even those who did no injustice but complacently enjoyed the privileges wrought by the injustice of others, that they were responsible to God. The prophets called kings and merchants and the whole society to account. We need contemporary prophets who "speak truth to power" on the environment, confronting governments and corporations that destroy and demean the creation. We need prophets who will call this society — and especially the churches — to repentance for the abuse of nature and its creatures and for the violation of a covenantal relationship with nature.

The prophets looked back to the past, saw in that past something of God's intentions, something of God's cause. And when God's cause was not honored by the people, they spoke in judgment. The story and the creation itself display something of God's cause, and prophets today call us to honor it.

The prophets were advocates for the poor. The story still nurtures voices raised as advocates for the poor, but it also may nurture voices raised as advocates for the earth. We need prophets who raise their voices in protest against "those who destroy the earth" (Rev. 11:18) and in solidarity with God's groaning creation. We need advocates for those creatures who cannot effectively speak up for their interests, whether giants of the sea like sperm whales or little creepy-crawly things like dung beetles, not to mention the earth itself.

Prudence: The Voice of the Sage

The Hebrew sage spoke a different language than the prophet, but it was still the language of faith. The wisdom teacher appealed less often to covenant. The voice of the sage was the voice of experience, the voice of one who had carefully observed the ways of human beings and of nature. The sage would distill from experience and observation principles at work in the world, principles to which it was both prudent and moral to conform. The wisdom of the sage could not be reduced to knowledge, but it surely called for learning — and for attitudes and acts appropriate to the principles at work in the world.

The sages of Israel carefully observed the ways of nature. The contemporary sage still learns wisdom by experience (like Wendell Berry, for example), but wisdom still calls for learning, for studying nature and its intricate relationships. Wisdom today will urge that some at least study the science of ecology. Such research and study should not reduce nature to a mere object. There is no wisdom there. But set in the context of faith in the Creator and delight in God's creation, such study might help us all to learn how to care for the creation a little better. Such study may even be oriented not just to mastery but also to wonder.

The sages warned against folly. Folly is the way that leads

to disaster. We need contemporary sages who will warn against the ecological folly we have followed for too long now. The sage invites us to learn a little wisdom before it is too late. To ignore, for example, the scientific evidence concerning global warming is the way of folly. The way of wisdom is the way of prudence. We need the contemporary sage who can remind us that human beings are, after all, a part of the creation, a part of the ecosystem of a particular place, and that its destruction is their destruction, its abasement is their abasement. Human beings do not — and cannot — live in some other world of spiritual or technological transcendence. Whatever the abuses, creation finally comes around to diminish the lives of the abusers, too. If we do not learn to care for the creation, then the creation itself will not care for us finally. Little wonder, then, that the sage can join the voice of wisdom to the voice of the prophets.

The voice of prudence calls for revising our practices and our politics, and there are some who say it is the most effective voice we have (at least in the short term — and the short term may be all the time we have). But the horror stories about the future in a world of changed climate and the barrage of scientific evidence of disasters befalling water, land, and air are evidently not enough to call us to responsibility. Surely our fears can motivate us; our anxiety about generations yet unborn (if they are to be born) can prompt change; prudence can guide us. But we also need voices calling us not just to prudence but to a vision of the reconciliation of human beings — with God and with each other, but also with the rest of nature, voices calling us to "a more excellent way." That more excellent way would still be love, to care for the creation out of love for the Creator and to care for creatures because they too are our neighbors in this world.

Analytical Discourse

The story does not give us a code, and it does not give us moral theory. We also need those who work carefully on moral casuistry and on theoretical coherence. Neither of these can substitute for the story; they do not have the power to shape an *ethos* that a *mythos* has. But if we are to tell and live the story well, we also need those who practice what James Gustafson calls "ethical discourse," by which he means "basically philosophical modes of argument and analysis."[5]

The story itself prompts the desire not only to perform the story faithfully in our lives and in Christian community, not only to give witness to the story in the larger community, but also to communicate with and to make common cause with other members of the larger community who care about the environment. In order to do that, we need to be careful with our words and careful with the words of others. Our words make sense in the context of the story in which they find their meaning. The narrative provides the background of intelligibility for our words. With those who do not share the story, communication is not always easy. But because the Christian story includes a story of Pentecost, we need not think it is impossible either, given the grace of God.

It is not simply a matter of finding the same words, for we will all use words like "nature" and "justice" and "responsibility," but we will not necessarily mean the same thing by them or make the same associations with them. As we have seen, "nature" is a slippery word. It has quite different connotations for one formed by the myth of the Baconian project and

5. Gustafson, "Varieties of Moral Discourse," p. 53.

for one formed by the myth of Romanticism. And the case is no different with "justice" or "responsibility."

And it is not simply a matter of good "translation" from one vocabulary to the other. The Greek word *logos* is a good translation of the Hebrew word *dabar;* each means "word." But the associations are different; *logos* means "reason" as well as "word," and *dabar* means "act" as well as "word."

It is a matter of careful speech and careful listening, a patient readiness to clarify our own speech and an eagerness to understand the other well. It demands analytical discourse. We may hope, of course, to nudge another's understanding of "nature" a little in the direction of "creation." We may hope to nudge this society's understanding of "justice" a little in the direction of a justice that hears the cries of the poor and powerless and away from the commonplace understanding of justice as "maximum freedom" and legal entitlement. We may hope at least to make intelligible that all responsibility may be seen in the context of responsibility *to* God, and that the responsibility shapes our account of what we are responsible *for.* But we may also discover by attentive listening to the voices of others interested in the environment that we had not yet fully understood or well communicated or well performed the biblical narrative and its moral implications.

Careful ethical analysis is important, moreover, not just to the task of communication but also to the task of casuistry, of applying rules and principles to particular cases. Careful distinctions are more the work of analytical discourse than the work of prophets, but by the hard work of ethical analysis and careful casuistry we may all understand a little better precisely what is required of us.

Policy

Finally, I turn to policy discourse, to that discourse about what governments or corporations or other institutions should do or leave undone. Policy discourse always takes place within particular institutions and within particular circumstances. There are frequently competing interests and obligations, making consensus nearly impossible and compromise difficult.[6] Little wonder that politics has been called "the art of the possible" or that the prophets are seldom altogether satisfied with the results of policy deliberations.

The story may never be reduced to policy, but the same story that moves us to care for the creation should move some of us also to careful attention to policy. Care for the creation requires policy, and the Christian community needs to listen carefully not only to the prophets, not only to the sages, not only to the analysts, but also to those who engage in policy discourse and policy deliberation.

Here, too, the story must not be forgotten or neglected, nor the myths that shape our culture go unchallenged. The

6. This is no excuse, of course, for a refusal to engage in public deliberation and debate about policy, neither for the church nor for the United States Senate. On the day I was finishing the revision of these Jellema Lectures for publication, the *New York Times* reported that Republicans had brought Senate debate about the legislation to combat global warming "to a dead stop . . . by insisting that the clerk read every word of the 492-page bill" (June 5, 2008, A19). I am sure the bill was not without flaws. Prophetic voices suggested that it was too little too late, like shuffling the deck chairs on the *Titanic*. Senator Inhofe evidently thought that because his home state of Oklahoma had a cold snap that winter the evidence concerning global warming had been discredited. The Democrats were reported to be frustrated by this maneuver to put a stop to the conversation, and so should we all be.

myth of the Baconian project, for example, with its confidence in technology, may not be mentioned, but it shapes policy in this culture. So does the myth of the project of capitalism, with its confidence in free markets and its suspicion of regulation in the interests of the poor or the environment. And so, for that matter, has the Romantic myth with its readiness to compartmentalize life joined to its commendable concern for wilderness.

To remember the story will not rescue policy deliberation from ambiguity and compromise, but it may nudge policy a little in the direction of a policy that fits the story a little better. The orientations of which we have spoken point the direction for policy, too. It is impossible in this context, of course, to do anything more than give a few illustrations concerning ecological policy.[7]

First, it should be observed that a concern for the creation abuts almost every policy arena. Deliberation about almost any policy, whether local or national or international, should be accompanied by consideration of the ecological implications of that policy. The point reaches from local zoning policy to international trade policy. And it surely demands that the environmental horrors of war be considered by those who engage in foreign policy.

Second, although we have rejected the myth of the project of capitalism, there remain markets, and national and international regulations will work best where there are reasonable

---

7. I have here and there in the foregoing hinted at the direction I would propose we nudge policy with respect to "altering" nature in assisted reproductive technologies, genetic modification, and medical care. The interested reader is invited to consult *Reading the Bible in the Strange World of Medicine* (Grand Rapids: Eerdmans, 2003), in which I take up these issues more fully.

and realistic market incentives to encourage both appropriate "green" technological innovation and necessary limitations on technologies that threaten the environment and its creatures.

Third, the orientation toward "good news to the poor" should be reflected in the midst of economic and structural inequalities, whether nationally or internationally. Priority should be given nationally to correct those instances in which we have wronged both the environment and the poor at once. And internationally there should be policies in which the rich countries take "preemptive" environmental action before there is global agreement and in which the rich countries help poor countries implement environmental policies that do not sacrifice their hopes for improved standards of living among the poor.

These recommendations are, admittedly, a long way from policy, but I hope they display something of the relevance of the narrative to policy deliberation.

Conclusion and Beginning

Christian ethics proceeds by way of reminder. That is why remembering the story is essential. But narrative is not sufficient. The Christian community needs those who are skilled also in these other forms of discourse. If the churches are to honor their tradition and fulfill their vocation as communities of moral discourse, deliberation, and discernment,[8] they need to engage in all these forms of discourse and to set them

---

8. See Allen Verhey, *Remembering Jesus: Christian Community, Scripture, and the Moral Life* (Grand Rapids: Eerdmans, 2002), pp. 3-48.

all in the context of the story. Each is demanding in its own way, but none of them are sufficient. No one person is skilled in all of them. But thankfully different people in the community have different vocations and different gifts. We need each other and the distinctive contributions of storyteller, prophet, sage, analyst, and policy maker. By that variety of gifts the Christian community is enriched, and by that variety of gifts we may learn to care for God's creation a little more faithfully.

All of these forms of discourse, however, remain just words unless, like the Word, they take flesh. The story must be not only remembered but performed, not only told but lived. So where shall we begin?

You should begin where you are. Tend the little corner of God's good earth where you live. Delight in its goodness and fruitfulness. Care about it. Protect it. Be an advocate for it. Join your neighbors at church and in the community in common delight and in common advocacy. Give thanks to God.

A Note on Typologies for the Relation of God and Nature

Theologians have developed various typologies for considering the relationship of God and nature.

Claude Stewart[1] lists five models: (1) In a deistic model God is like the inventor and nature like a machine. (2) In a dialogic model the relationship is like the relationship of two persons. (3) In a monarchical model God is ruler and nature God's realm or subject. (4) In a process model God is to the world as an individual is to a community. And (5) in an agential model God is the agent and nature is God's actions. His own preference is for the agential model.[2]

Ian Barbour's typology[3] includes eight models: (1) the mo-

---

1. Claude Stewart, Jr., *Nature in Grace: A Study in the Theology of Nature* (Macon, GA: Mercer University Press, 1983).

2. Stewart, *Nature in Grace,* p. 281. For a cogent account of the agential model see Thomas Tracy, *God, Action, and Embodiment* (Grand Rapids: Eerdmans, 1984).

3. Ian Barbour, *Religion in an Age of Science* (San Francisco: Harper & Row, 1990), chapter 9.

narchical model, (2) the deist model, (3) a neo-Thomist model in which God is a craftsman and nature God's tool, (4) a kenotic model in which God is a parent to nature, the child, (5) an existentialist model in which God is person and nature an object, (6) a linguistic model (roughly equivalent to Stewart's agential model), (7) an embodiment model in which the world is the body of God,[4] and (8) a process model. Barbour prefers the process model.[5] The issues are complex, and some synthesis is probably required, but the story seems to suggest the plausibility of an agential model supplemented by monarchical and dialogic models.[6]

4. See Sallie McFague, *The Body of God: An Ecological Theology* (Minneapolis: Augsburg Fortress, 1993).

5. John Cobb is probably the best-known defender of the process model with respect to the relation of God and nature; see John Cobb, *Is It Too Late? A Theology of Ecology* (Beverly Hills, CA: Bruce, 1972).

6. See further Steven Bouma-Prediger, *The Greening of Theology: The Ecological Models of Rosemary Radford Ruether, Joseph Sittler, and Jürgen Moltmann* (Oxford: Oxford University Press, 2000), pp. 287-89.

APPENDIX B

A Note on Typologies for the Relation of Nature and Humanity

In addition to the typologies concerning the relation of God and nature (see Appendix A), some Christian theologians have provided typologies for the relation of humanity to nature and for the human vocation with respect to it.

For example, in an early and influential book in response to Lynn White, Jr., John Passmore distinguished two types, despotism and stewardship, and he argued that despotism owed more to Greek patterns of thought than to the biblical tradition.[1]

James Walters also distinguished two ideal-types, the "steward" and the "co-creator." The "steward" typically emphasizes conserving and preserving the creation, while the "co-creator" emphasizes the freedom to intervene in nature to alter it, to correct or "redeem" it.[2] He is surely right to claim

1. John Passmore, *Man's Responsibility for Nature* (London: Duckworth, 1974).

2. James J. Walter, "Theological Issues in Genetics," *Theological Studies* (March 1999): 124-39, especially pp. 124-29.

that "steward" typically emphasizes conserving and preserving the creation while "co-creator" emphasizes the freedom to intervene in nature to correct or "redeem" it. Both, however, are responsible to God. One might well talk of the creativity of good stewards or the stewardship of responsible co-creators (preserving existing goods). Frankly, I do not think a whole lot is at stake in the name we give to our vocation — if we set it in the context of the biblical story! Both "steward" and "co-creator" are responsible to God in the story, and in that responsibility the good steward will be called to creativity and the responsible co-creator will be called to preserve existing goods. More is at stake, I think, in whether our role, as steward or as co-creator, is oriented by the myths of genetic reductionism, the Baconian project, the liberal project, the market, Romanticism, or by the wisdom of the remembered story.

A richer typology has been provided by James M. Gustafson. In *A Sense of the Divine,* he distinguished these ideal-types: despotism, dominion, stewardship, subordination, and participation.[3]

The first ideal-type is "despotism." In this ideal-type "the natural environment can be exploited arbitrarily by humans for whatever ends they choose or perceive to be of immediate benefit to them" (p. 79). This is the ideal-type associated with the Baconian project. Nature has no intrinsic value; it is raw material or a tool for human use; it is desacralized and commodified; or it is a threatening monster that not only may be but also must be mastered. And humanity has be-

3. James M. Gustafson, *A Sense of the Divine: The Natural Environment from a Theocentric Perspective* (Cleveland: Pilgrim Press, 1998), pp. 77-106. (The page references in parentheses in the next few paragraphs are references to this work.)

come a god, or if a place for God is preserved, then humanity has been authorized to be "God's sovereign viceroy over nature." Human capacities to control nature may not yet have achieved the omniscience and omnipotence ascribed to God, but they are steadily increasing. Gustafson acknowledges that Christian (as well as non-Christian) thinkers have sometimes attempted to justify this account of the relation of humanity to nature, but he regards it as deeply flawed. It empties the world of mystery; it makes an idol of human technological power; and it gives a distorted image of God's rule (pp. 85-87).

Gustafson's second ideal-type is "dominion." This, of course, is the language of Genesis 1. (And the name for this type may be regretted for this very reason, for it gives the impression that this ideal-type is the "biblical" model.) Although such language has sometimes been taken to authorize despotism, as in Lynn White's essay, Gustafson thinks it must be distinguished from "despotism." Whereas "despotism assumes sovereign ownership and thus implies the right to use nature arbitrarily," "dominion" recognizes God's ownership. Nature on this view is not sacred, but it is a "gift" or a "loan" from God. Nature is not God, but it is — and remains — God's. The "gift" is not a legal transfer of title to ownership. Moreover, it is a *good* gift. Dominion recognizes the natural environment and all of life as a gift from the goodness of God. God created all things and saw that they were good, indeed very good. In this religious context receiving a gift evokes not only gratitude for it but also a sense of responsibility for its care and use (p. 91). "And use" must be added, because in this ideal-type there is a recognition of "the appropriateness of the use of nature . . . for human life and activity" (p. 91). The religious thinkers whom Gustafson regards as exemplars of this ideal-type, Karl Barth and Martin Buber, are instructive. Karl Barth eschews the nature mysticism that, in his view, marks Albert Schweitzer's proposal of "reverence for life," and he proposes instead an attitude of "respect for life." This respect will not be empty of religious "awe" before the natural world, but it will be empty of idolatry. It will authorize the use of nature for human wellbeing — but as "a priestly act," a sacrifice of great religious and moral significance. Buber, in the possibility of an I-Thou relation with nature, infuses the human relation to nature with an aura of mystery that might make Barth nervous, but like Barth, Buber recognizes the appropriateness of an I-it relation to nature and the use of nature for human wellbeing.

"Stewardship" is Gustafson's third ideal-type. It bears a resemblance to his second ideal-type (and is regarded by its exemplars as an interpretation of the biblical language of "dominion"). Stewardship emphasizes that the ultimate authority, the dominion, if you will, is retained by God. Human beings are God's stewards (or deputies, or agents), authorized by God but always answerable to God. They are to act on God's behalf and in the service of God's purposes and causes. The exemplar here is Douglas John Hall, *Imaging God: Dominion as Stewardship,* but Gustafson believes this model to be "the preferred way of understanding man's responsibilities for nature in Judaism and Christianity" (p. 92). Human beings are both identified with nature and differentiated from it, but the differentiation is precisely this vocation or function of "steward" in relation to the rest of creation. It is not that the rest of creation is "useful" for human beings but that human beings are charged to be caretakers for the rest.

Gustafson's fourth ideal-type is "subordination." This ideal-type is, according to Gustafson, more characteristic of

Eastern religious traditions than of Western religious traditions. He cites Joseph Kitagawa's summary comparison:

> In contrast to the contemplation of western peoples meditation in the east tends to be directed toward sacred reality present in nature. This is due to the fact that unlike their western counterparts, who believe themselves to be situated somewhere between God and the world of nature, eastern people have always accepted the humble role of being a part of the world of nature.[4]

In this type humans are "subservient to the regulative order or inner balance of the cosmos, variously known as *Rta, Dharma,* and *Tao*."[5] In its extreme form "subordination" would seem to reject any human intervention in nature, but even hunter-gatherers intervene in the natural environment. This ideal-type affirms a natural equilibrium or balance or harmony that provides norms for human performance. The challenges, of course, are to identify and establish the equilibrium. According to Gustafson, Albert Schweitzer comes closest to this ideal-type in Western religious literature, with his call to "enter the service of the creative will whence all life emanates" by "serving every kind of life."[6]

Gustafson's fifth ideal-type, and the one he commends, is

4. Joseph M. Kitagawa, *The History of Religions: Understanding Human Experience* (Atlanta: Scholars Press, 1987), p. 246; cited in Gustafson, *A Sense of the Divine,* p. 77.

5. Gustafson, *A Sense of the Divine,* p. 78, citing Kitagawa, *The History of Religions,* p. 246.

6. Albert Schweitzer, "The Ethics of Reverence for Life," in Henry Clark, *The Ethical Mysticism of Albert Schweitzer* (Boston: Beacon Press, 1962), p. 189; cited in Gustafson, *A Sense of the Divine,* p. 97.

"participation." "Nothing exists independently; everything exists interdependently" (p. 99). Humans participate in and depend upon the patterns and processes of the interdependence of life in the world. There is a religious dimension to the senses of dependence on the environment and interdependence with it and to the sense of the contingency of our lives and of the natural world. Those senses, Gustafson says, are present in all the world's religions and in the "natural piety" of secular persons (p. 101). Our participation and interdependence do not require non-intervention. On the contrary, "we can and should intervene for the sake of humans and nature itself" (p. 103). God is at work in the patterns and processes to make possible human wellbeing and the wellbeing of other things, but God does not "guarantee" the human good. Human beings must work out some provisional priorities, valuing aspects of nature not only in relation to individual and more general human interests but also in relation to the "interests" of other parts of the natural world, remembering that human life is dependent not only upon the processes of nature but also upon intentional human participation in them (p. 103). There is no way to avoid moral ambiguity or the reality of conflict among the "interests" of the different parts, but we must make an effort to relate the good of each part to the good of the whole and to act on the maxim, "Act so that you consider all things never only as a means to your ends, or even to collective human ends" (p. 106).

It seems to me that the stewardship model has much to commend it within the biblical narrative, but it is not without its problems. The fundamental problem is that stewardship is too frequently regarded as a kind of "property management." We are stewards by managing another's property. It may not be our property by "gift" or even on "loan" as in the "dominion" model, but it slips toward that model. When we think of our responsibility as "stewardship," as "property management," we distort, first, the relation of God to the world, as though the relation of God to the world were simply owner to property. The relation of God to the world is much more "personal" — and mutually responsive — than that. And then we distort, secondly, our relation to the world, as if it were simply the property of another for which we must give an account on a day of reckoning. Gustafson's fifth model does not have the same weakness, but it seems to me not sufficiently attentive to the responsibility of human creatures *to* God and to loyalty to the cause of God as that may be discerned from the biblical story. That responsibility *to* God is surely appropriately underscored in the stewardship model. So, how shall we think and speak of our responsibility to God for nature? I think "responsibility" itself is the best word and the best image.

Name Index

Name Index

Fudpucker, Wilhelm, 52n.6

Gilbert, Walter, 17-18
Gilkey, Langdon, 106n.58
Granberg-Michaelson, Wes,
 69n.5
Gregorios, Paulos, 1 n.1, 12n.10
Gustafson, James M., 65, 68n.4,
 119n.1, 128n.5, 137-41

Hall, Douglas J., 80n.24, 139
Hamer, Dean, 20n.17
Hanson, Mark, 25n.27, 97n.48
Harrison, Peter, 52n.6, 53n.9,
 55nn.14,15, 57, 59
Hartt, Julian, 83n.32
Hobbes, Thomas, 8
Hofrichter, Richard, 113n.64
Hudson, Horace F., 17n.8

Irenaeus, 53

Jellema, W. Harry, vii-viii, 39
Jonas, Hans, 23

Kaufmann, Gordon, 1n.1,
 12n.10
Keenan, James F., 18n.13
Kierkegaard, Søren, 97
Kitagawa, Joseph M., 140n.4

LaHaye, Tim, 117n.68
Lappe, Marc, 37n.39
Lash, Nicholas, 108n.60
Lebacqz, Karen, 34n.35
Lewis, C. S., 1-8, 75-76, 108n.60
Lindee, Susan, 17n.10, 18, 20
Lindsey, Hal, 117n.68

Lyotard, Jean-François, 33n.33,
 34n.34

MacDonald, George, 108
Macquarrie, John, 107n.58
Marcion, 65-66
Marcus Aurelius, 4
McFague, Sally, 137n.4
McKenny, Gerald, 22nn.18,19
McKibben, Bill, 75n.12
Meilaender, Gilbert, 29n.29
Midgley, Mary, 15
Miller, Patrick D., Jr., 76n.17
Miller-Travis, Vernice, 113n.64
Moltmann, Jürgen, 69n.5
Monod, Jacques, 14-15
Moule, C. F. D., 108n.62
Murphy, Charles M., 52n.7

Nagel, Thomas, 60n.23
Nelkin, Dorothy, 17n.10, 18, 20
Newsom, Carol, 75n.12
Niebuhr, H. Richard, 68n.3
Niebuhr, Reinhold, 97
Nietzsche, Friedrich, 57

O'Donovan, Oliver, 106n.57
Oelschlaeger, Max, 39-40, 44

Parmenides, 2
Passmore, John, 136
Peters, Ted, 15, 20n.16
Plato, 3
Pope, Alexander, 8

Quam, Robert, 12n.10
Quash, Ben, 124n.4

Reinders, Hans, 26n.28, 30

Subject Index

Scripture Index